Ancient Magick for
Today's Witch Series

CRYSTAL MAGICK

MONIQUE JOINER SIEDLAK

oshunpublications.com

Crystal Magick © Copyright 2020 by Monique Joiner Siedlak

ISBN 978-1-950378-43-2 (Paperback)

ISBN 978-1-961362-24-6 (Hardback)

ISBN 978-1-950378-42-5 (eBook)

All rights reserved

The content contained within this book may not be reproduced, duplicated or transmitted without direct written permission from the author or the publisher.

Under no circumstances will any blame or legal responsibility be held against the publisher, or author, for any damages, reparation, or monetary loss due to the information contained within this book, either directly or indirectly.

Legal Notice

This book is copyright protected. It is only for personal use. You cannot amend, distribute, sell, use, quote or paraphrase any part, or the content within this book, without the consent of the author or publisher.

Disclaimer Notice

Please note the information contained within this document is for educational and entertainment purposes only. All effort has been executed to present accurate, up to date, reliable, complete information. No warranties of any kind are declared or implied. Readers acknowledge that the author is not engaged in the rendering of legal, financial, medical or professional advice. The content within this book has been derived from various sources. Please consult a licensed professional before attempting any techniques outlined in this book.

By reading this document, the reader agrees that under no circumstances is the author responsible for any losses, direct or indirect, that are incurred as a result of the use of the information contained within this document, including, but not limited to, errors, omissions, or inaccuracies.

Cover Design by MJS

Cover Images by MidJourney

Published by Oshun Publications

www.oshunpublications.com

ANCIENT MAGICK FOR TODAY'S WITCH SERIES

The *Ancient Magick for Today's Witch Series* is a series for modern witches to explore ancient magick, covering Celtic, Gypsy, and Crystal magic, among others. It offers practical advice on spells, rituals, and enchantments for today's use, incorporating natural energies and spiritual connections. With insights into Shamanism, Wicca, and more, it helps readers enhance their magickal journey, offering paths to protection, prosperity, and spiritual growth by combining ancient wisdom with contemporary practice.

Wiccan Basics

Candle Magick

Wiccan Spells

Love Spells

Abundance Spells

Herb Magick

Moon Magick

Creating Your Own Spells

Gypsy Magic

Protection Magick

Celtic Magick

Shamanic Magick

Crystal Magic

Sacred Spaces

Solitary Witchcraft

Novice Witch's Guide

MONIQUE JOINER SIEDLAK

GET UPDATES, FREEBIES & GIVEAWAYS

JOIN MY NEWSLETTER

MOJOSIEDLAK.COM/MOONLIGHT-MUSINGS

CONTENTS

Introduction	xiii
1. History of Crystals, Rocks, and Stones	1
2. The Difference	9
3. Where to Start	13
4. Energies	27
5. Crystals to Use in Magic	31
6. Spells	59
7. Talismans	71
Conclusion	79
References	83
About the Author	91
More Books by Monique	93
Don't Miss Out	97

INTRODUCTION

Magic and its practice have been around for thousands of years. Before people of Northern and Western Europe started converting to Christianity, they followed the pagan way of life. They held strong beliefs in the power of nature. They practiced the freedom to decide what they wanted to believe in and the worship of gods and goddesses.

These people celebrated and followed traditions in the ways of the old. They worshiped their ancestors and those who came before, practicing magic and partaking in magical traditions. They had a deeply held belief in an afterlife that awaited them after departing from this physical world.

Pagan beliefs were practiced all around the globe. Many societies were untouched by Christian influence. When a man named Gerald Gardner traveled in Asia, he became interested in the magical practices, ancient traditions, and occult beliefs of these pagan individuals. When he returned home to England, he founded the Wiccan way of life, which is also known today as "modern paganism" or "witchcraft."

After he wrote and published a book on witchcraft, it became quite popular in the United States. Well-received in many countries, Wicca soon spread far and wide. In today's modern age, the Wiccan way of life and magic has become the norm. The Wiccan movement has grown significantly since it was first founded by Gardner in the 1930s.

Today, we observe seven different types of magic practiced by Wiccans, namely binding magic, candle magic, crystal magic, dream magic, elemental magic, glamor magic, and herbal magic. The most popular types of magic are candle magic, crystal magic, and herbal magic.

Crystals are incredible stones of power that are formed in the earth and help stabilize your mind, body, and spirit, as well as cleanse your chakras. They also provide the person using or wearing them with various benefits, such as protection, wealth, luck, and health.

The positive effects that are provided by that particular stone will depend on the properties and attributes of it. For example, suppose a stone has healing and calming qualities. In that case, it will heal you emotionally and physically and remove stress and anxiety from your life.

This book is perfect for anyone who is just starting their journey with crystal magic. Perhaps does not know where to begin, or for anyone who is merely thinking of trying it out. Crystal magic is not difficult. I consider it to be one of the more natural types of magic that you can practice. Focusing mostly on meditating with a candle and the crystals. Visualizing your intentions and what outcome you would like from the spell.

Once you get the hang of handling crystals in simple spells and creating charms, this practice will immediately develop into a natural part of your life. Crystals can be used in all aspects of your life. From trying to improve your fertility, you can become pregnant to help you overcome obsessive-compulsive disorders and addictions. They can even help you communicate more effectively with other people.

In this book, I will be introducing you to the history of crystals, rocks, and stones. I will reveal to you how you can create your crystal collection, stick to a budget when buying crystals, and what to look out for when you go into an occult store or buy online.

Additionally, I will provide you with some information regarding how to cleanse your crystals and how to program and activate them. Finally, I will introduce you to thirteen of the most commonly used crystals and stones and some simple spells that you can try to get you started.

Let your journey commence!

1
HISTORY OF CRYSTALS, ROCKS, AND STONES

We use crystals in our everyday lives, such as decorations, medicine, computer monitors, television screens, satellites, cell phones, solar-powered devices, and transformers that move electricity from one place to another, beauty products, jewelry, and even food. Crystals are everywhere. But how are crystals formed, and how have they been used throughout history?

Crystals, rocks, and stones have been used throughout history, from the earliest Sumerian civilizations. They have been utilized in different ways, depending on the cultures and traditions that people followed. Today, Western influence has dramatically helped shape these gems into powerful stones that can absorb energy, amplify power, and provide the person who is using or wearing them with protection, healing, and guidance.

Early Civilizations

Before history was recorded, everything that happened within a tribe or a society of importance was passed down verbally from one generation to the next. Because of this, it is difficult to pinpoint with certainty exactly when people first began using crystals, rocks, and stones for their various properties and purposes.

The Sumerians in Mesopotamia are recorded as the earliest known civilizations to utilize crystals for protection and healing. They began to do so from as early as 4000 BCE. The Sumerians would use gypsum and hematite, which are softer than other crystals, to create cylinder seals with engraved images that indicated a person's social class, events that occurred, and religious ceremonies.

These depictions on the cylinder seals would be transferred by rolling them over wet clay. Its impression would be placed inside temples and used in religious ceremonies.

Ancient Egypt

The ancient Egyptians' beliefs were heavily intertwined with crystals and the other elements. Ancient Egyptian royalty would wear stones and crystals like carnelian, clear quartz, emeralds, lapis lazuli, and turquoise embedded in their amulets, crowns, ornaments, and jewelry. They did this to show honor and respect for their gods and goddesses. Stones and crystals were used for health and protection. They were also used in burial objects, as well as in religious ceremonies.

Lapis lazuli, a dark blue gem with flecks of gold, was one of the most common and well-treasured stones. It was set in amulets and crowns of the Egyptian royals. Lapis lazuli was associated with a higher social class, like pharaohs and judges, and it held religious significance in their rites and rituals. When these items were worn on the ancient Egyptians' forehead between their eyebrows and over their third eye chakra, it could provide the wearer with powers of divination and spiritual enlightenment. When worn elsewhere on the body, the lapis lazuli would help a person have good luck and become more confident.

Similarly, some Egyptians were buried with quartz placed on their foreheads or embedded in their face masks. These masks were put over their face before their coffin was sealed. These quartz crystals provided the wearer with guidance and a safe journey as they crossed over into the afterlife. They also ensured that their soul's Ba and Ka energies are balanced and at peace with one another when that happened.

In addition to these ways in which the ancient Egyptians used stones and crystals in their lives, they would also grind up crystals like galena, malachite, and rose quartz into a powder substance to create makeup and other cosmetics. These concoctions made the ancient Egyptians look good and also provided them with medicinal and spiritual benefits.

Galena, also known as "kohl," was applied extensively to the eyes as an eyeliner. At the same time, malachite was crushed to create a colorful powder that could be used on or under their eyelids and across their brow bone. The ancient Egyptians used eye makeup from these crystals to make themselves appear more powerful and provide them with protection. Rose quartz was used in creams and other facial cosmetics to help prevent the wearer from developing wrinkles as they got older.

Ancient Greece

The beliefs and mythologies of the ancient Greeks contributed to the most knowledge that we have of crystals today compared to other civilizations. The word crystal in Greek means "ice crystal," The Greeks believed that clear quartz crystals were pieces of ice that would stay frozen forever and not melt.

The ancient Greeks gave crystals most of the names that we know them by today. They used different ones throughout their lives, from their daily events and happenings to fighting on the battlefield. Some common crystals that they used were amethysts and hematites. The Greeks also associated crystals and stones with their gods and goddesses.

Amethysts are beautiful crystals and are strongly associated with the ancient Greeks and their mythologies. The word "amethystos," which is the Greek word for amethyst, was described as meaning "not drunken." Amethysts first received their name from the mythological story of the god Dionysus and goddess Diana.

The Greek god Dionysus became angry with a young woman named Amethyst. When Amethyst went to the goddess Diana to ask for help, the goddess turned her into a clear white crystal to provide the woman with protection. When Dionysus felt remorse for what he had done to the woman, he cried into his chalice until it overflowed and stained the clear stone a purple color.

Wine and alcoholic beverages were consumed heavily in the ancient Greeks' times and would be included with most meals. The ancient Greeks believed that by adorning their cups and chalices with amethysts, they would enjoy more wine and alcohol and be protected against becoming drunk or developing a hangover later or the next day.

Hematite was also a well-known crystal that the ancient Greeks used. The word "haematites lithos," which is the Greek word for the hematite crystal, is defined as meaning "bloodstone." The hematite stone was made of iron ore and received its name because it would turn a red-pigmented color or give off a red sheen when it was exposed to oxygen.

Aries, the Greek god of war, was associated with iron; therefore, this stone became associated with Aries as well. When Greek soldiers went into battle, they would crush hematite and form a paste that they would rub on their skin. They assumed that it would protect them in battle. Some soldiers also ground up other crystals that had protective or courageous qualities before they went into battle.

Crystal amulets of various types were often worn by Greek sailors, who believed that the crystals and stones' properties would protect them on their voyages and from the mythological beasts of the ocean.

Ancient China

There were a few different stones and crystals that the ancient Chinese used. The most well-known and well-favored stone that the Chinese still use to this day is the jade crystal. It was used for its many different properties, such as healing and protection. Jade was also used to decorate musical instruments and decorative ornaments. The ancient Chinese also crafted armor made from it and would place them onto their emperors when they were buried.

Several ancient Chinese also believed that jade was a useful healing crystal that could protect their organs, specifically the kidneys. The jade crystal would reduce their risk of developing kidney-related diseases or infections or decrease their effects if they were already suffering from it. They also believed that this crystal provided them with protection and would prevent them from experiencing bad luck.

There were also a variety of other healing crystals that the ancient Chinese made use of in their medicines and even in their alternative healing practices, such as acupuncture. Acupuncture was first used in China in 100 BCE, where thread-thin needles were placed into specific points in a person's body to help relieve pain. To make this healing process more effective, the ancient Chinese would use needles with crystal tips.

The Chinese contributed heavily towards a modern understanding of the use of crystals in healing and for protection. They also associated certain stones and crystals with the zodiac signs and the different phases of the moon.

The Middle Ages

In the Middle Ages, between 300 CE and 1500 CE, the properties of stones and crystals, their uses, roles, and where they came from, were researched and explored. When people began to examine the stones during this time, they would record all of the information they gleaned from them into tomes. These would cover the topic of stones and crystals in great detail. From their spiritual and metaphysical properties to how they were able to treat and decrease their risk of developing certain health conditions depending on the stone. They also looked at how they could improve one's mental health.

During this time, many people would embed crystals and gemstones into amulets and their weapons, armors, and other clothing pieces. These crystals and gemstones were both used for decorative purposes and to protect the wearer.

However, when Christianity came to Europe in the Middle Ages, the church did not agree with the Europeans' ancient spiritual practices, which included the use of stones and crystals for their healing and protective qualities, despite references in the Bible to using healing gems. When Europeans were gradually converted to Christianity, many gave up what they once knew and moved away from these practices to appease the church.

In the Bible, there are many mentions of healing stones and crystals. Still, none are as crucial as the breastplate worn by the high priest, which is mentioned in Exodus. This breastplate was adorned with twelve gemstones that symbolized the twelve Israeli tribes.

These gemstones included ruby, topaz, beryl, turquoise, sapphire, emerald, jacinth, agate, amethyst, chrysolite, onyx, and jasper. These were used for their various properties and benefits, like their abilities to heal and to protect the twelve tribes.

Modern Day

During the Renaissance period in Europe between the 14th and 17th centuries, the healing and medicinal properties of stones and crystals resurfaced to help prevent and treat different medical conditions. When people used these stones and crystals in conjunction with concocted herbal medicines, they could recover from their sicknesses at a much more accelerated rate. They also provided the wearer with protection from the disease and the strength to fight it.

With this rebirth of the use of healing crystals, people began to cleanse their stones and crystals before they used or wore them to ensure that they were not inhabited by demons and evil spirits.

However, the use of crystals for healing and medicine did not last long. In the early 1600s, a man who wrote about precious stones named Thomas Nicols claimed that gemstones did not have any healing or medicinal qualities, because they were only objects. After this, many people lost interest in crystals and gemstones and stopped utilizing them.

In the mid-19th century, people developed new interests in stones and crystals with a shift towards new ways of thinking in a changing world. People became captivated by spirituality, astrology, and the occult, the movement of energy, the vibrations of crystals and gemstones, and the power and influence of positive and negative thoughts.

These new practices and sciences have been researched and studied extensively by scientists and researchers. Their findings have paved a new way of life were using stones and crystals have become the norm, combining previous knowledge that was known on the subjects. While the movement towards this new era of spirituality and beliefs took some time for people to accept, we now see crystals used in cultures and religions worldwide.

Today, there is an amalgamation of all the different ways of viewing and using stones and crystals. They provide healing benefits, which are now incorporated into alternative forms of healing like meditation, reiki, and even yoga. Using stones and crystals to cast spells of protection over our loved ones - or fertility spells to help you become more likely to conceive.

Many people walk around with bracelets embedded with stones and crystals like amethyst, rhodonite, and onyx that help to curb the anxiety and stress of the modern world. Talismans have also become a big part of our lives, and rings and stones are often engraved with runes, images, or words that can bring us protection and good luck.

2
THE DIFFERENCE

To understand how we use crystals in magic, we should first grasp what crystals are and what makes them different from stones, rocks, minerals, and geodes. When we write or speak about crystals, we often use the terms "crystal" and "stone" interchangeably. This is because there are not that many differences between them, so people generally believe them to be the same.

The most essential component that makes up crystals, stones, and rocks is a mineral. A mineral is defined as being an organic substance that occurs in nature. The chemical atoms that are contained within it are arranged into a specific repeating pattern, depending on which type of mineral has been created.

Some minerals are crystalline, meaning that they can crystallize and form small, or even microscopic, crystal structures inside the rock. Other minerals are mineraloid. These do not crystallize or form any crystal structure. An example of a mineraloid is amber, a resin created by trees that we use to preserve items like flowers, bugs, and so on.

There are also times when rocks are split open, and there is a cavity inside it that is lined with crystals like quartz, agate, amethysts, and calcite. These rocks are called geodes. Because the crystals grow inside the geode, these crystals are not disrupted by the wear and tear that occurs to the other rocks. These crystals stay in excellent condition.

There are thousands of diverse types of minerals. Each one has its own composition of chemicals and internal structures that make it different from others. Some common examples of minerals are amphibole, calcite, feldspar, halite, mica, and quartz.

Meanwhile, a rock is made up of one or more different types of minerals. Some are only made of one single mineral, but the majority contain more. For example, granite, a commonly found rock, is made up of the minerals feldspar, mica, and quartz. A rock is often found to be much larger than a stone. Some common examples of rocks are basalt, granite, limestone, sandstone, and schist.

There are three specific types of rocks that you will encounter, particularly, igneous, sedimentary, and metamorphic rocks. Igneous or volcanic rocks form when liquid magma solidifies by cooling down. Igneous rocks can cool down above ground, such as when a volcano has erupted, or slowly underground.

Sedimentary rocks are created when the remnants of other rocks are left behind on the surface. They are covered by other rocks and sediments. Metamorphic rocks are formed when igneous or sedimentary rocks have been transformed in some way through heat, pressure, or reactive fluids. It's changing the minerals contained within the rock and thereby creating a new type of rock.

A stone is a non-metallic mineral that is cut from a larger piece of rock. A rock is often too large to move on its own. It is cut down into more manageable rock fragments and then reduced to smaller stones that can be moved more quickly. Another difference between a rock and a stone is that a rock can be hard or soft. It depends on the minerals that have been combined. In contrast, a stone is only a hard substance. Stones can be brought in their rough, raw form, but can also be cut down further, polished, or tumbled.

A crystal is a solid mass of atoms of the same type of minerals that combine to form a repeating pattern that provides the crystal with its shape and internal structure. Rocks and stones are made up of small, sometimes microscopic crystals, but often you will find that crystals grow larger in form when the right conditions are met. The term "crystal" is commonly used by people who use rocks and minerals for their healing purposes.

Crystals are created when a hot liquid cools down and crystallizes, which is the process by which a crystal is formed and grown. There are a few distinct ways a liquid can crystallize. Each method, as well as the available materials in the immediate environment, dictates the crystal's structure, how it functions, and what properties it provides to the person using or wearing the crystal.

Some crystals form when hot magma beneath the earth's surface cools down, and pressure is applied during the crystallization process. This creates a tough material that is difficult to cut and polish without the correct tools. These include diamonds, rubies, and emeralds.

Other crystals are formed when a liquid evaporates and combines with materials of the same type to create a crystal. An excellent example of this is a salt crystal. When salt water evaporates into the atmosphere, the salt's particles will accumulate and crystallize, forming a salt crystal.

Some crystals can be formed by dripping down into caves and deep caverns. In this method, the hot liquid begins to cool and crystallize as it runs down the rocks and structures in caves and caverns. These ore veins slowly build up over time, and stalagmite crystals can be formed.

Stalagmites are often found on the roof inside a cave or cavern. It forms when the liquid has accumulated on the room and crystallized, along with columns, or on any vertical structure that supports the roof of the cave. This runoff runs down these structures. This can also form large deposits on the ground of the cave from liquid dripping down that can grow quite tall over time.

3
WHERE TO START

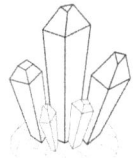

So, you are interested in starting your crystal collection, learning how to cast spells, and creating talismans to improve your life and well-being. Choosing a crystal might seem like a daunting task at first. After all, there are so many to choose from. having said that, this does not have to be a challenging choice.

When deciding upon your crystal, you should look at what you need in your life at this moment in time. Ask yourself what outcome you are expecting to bring about through using the crystal you are about to buy. For example, if you are looking to find a partner, you should consider getting yourself rose quartz.

While it can seem exciting to have an extensive crystal collection, you should remember that there are hundreds of crystals out there. Many of them share similar properties and characteristics. If you buy one crystal that embodies the qualities and benefits that you are looking for, then this is better than having many that do similar things.

You should also remember that your collection will grow over time, so you do not need to buy several initially. First, focus on purchasing one or two crystals that speak to you, and then come back another time.

Below, I have provided some helpful information about buying crystals on a budget and how you can go about cleansing, programming, and activating your precious new objects. These steps are essential to ensure that your crystals are performing optimally in your magic practices.

Crystals on a Budget

Buying and investing in crystals does not have to be an expensive endeavor that leaves you out of pocket. There are plenty of ways you can save money while still determining quality crystals and gemstones.

When you are seeking to establish your stone and crystal collection for the first time, you should take some time to see what you are looking for. What do you need your crystal(s) to do for you? For example, if your objective is to develop courage or perform a spell to build up your bravery, you should first look at first getting a tiger's eye.

You do not need to buy twenty different stones and crystals right off the bat, and I do not suggest that you approach crystal buying in this way at all, as stated earlier. You can start your collection by just buying one gemstone at a time as needed or becoming familiar with it. When your needs change, or if you have done some research and find that you require a different gemstone for a specific spell or use as a charm, you can move on to the next one.

When buying stones and crystals, it is recommended that you shop around a bit and find out about the different occult stores near you that sell gemstones. You can also buy stones and crystals from Amazon, but I prefer to go into a shop to get a sense for the atmosphere that the gemstones are in.

If you are buying crystals on a budget, I do not suggest that you decide to buy from the first place that has the lowest prices. You might find that their stones and crystals are not of good quality or may not feel connected to any of the stones in the shop.

It is essential to take some time and walk around a shop to look at the different gemstones that they have on offer while also considering the price. If one shop has a crystal that you want for $15 and you do not feel connected to it, or the quality is not good. Still, another store has a crystal for $19, and you sense a link to it, then you should opt for the more expensive crystal you know will work for you.

There are many stones and crystals out there that sell for under $20. You should keep your eyes peeled for good deals when browsing for gemstones while also bearing quality and connection in mind. I strongly suggest that you avoid shops that sell stones and crystals for extravagant amounts, even if you are not buying on a budget.

You can start with some excellent stones and crystals. This including basic quartz, rose quartz, amethyst, citrine, moonstone, carnelian, bloodstone, jade, lapis lazuli, malachite, tiger's eye, jet, and hematite. If you are struggling to choose one, then look at Chapter 5 in this book at the different properties of each one. You can also read about some of the spells that have been included in this book in Chapter 6. There you will get a feel for what type of spell you want to cast over yourself and others.

Choosing and Being Chosen

When you are choosing a crystal for the first time, it's important to remember to avoid choosing your crystal; instead, it, in fact, chooses you. You could go into a shop and look at the quality of the stone or crystal and decide to buy it without feeling connected to the gemstone. However, your stone or crystal might not act in the way you want it to, or it may not be as useful in the spells that you cast. It is essential to find a gemstone that speaks to you and your soul.

If you are buying your stones and crystals from a physical store, you should walk into the shop and walk around to first get a feel for the store. Some might leave you feeling empty, and others can make you feel like you have stepped into your own home. If you do not feel comfortable in the store, you can still stay to have a look at the crystals, but it is better to buy them from a place that makes you feel at ease.

Once you find the perfect store, you should go to where they keep their stones and crystals and close your eyes as you touch the surface and different facets of each gemstone. If one feels familiar to you, you should open your eyes and examine the various crystals of the same type that are laid out in front of you.

Next, you should visualize or think to yourself what you want your crystal to do for you or what properties you would like in it. Suppose you are anxious, and you want one that can help you de-stress and stop worrying or one that you can use to cast spells to reduce your anxieties and worries. In that case, you may be drawn to amethyst or rose quartz crystal. Frequently, a shop will label each stone or crystal type with its specific properties, making your search for the right one a bit easier.

You might feel the stone or crystal's energy pull at you to pick it up and hold its weight in your hands. It might be the same crystal that you previously felt, or it could be different altogether. No matter which it is, make sure that it feels right to you and that you have looked at all the others.

You may also find that your eyes are drawn to a specific crystal; this is another way that it can call to you. Make sure that you don't ignore any feelings that you have during this time, and select the one that speaks to you the most.

When choosing and buying online from stores like Amazon, the process of selecting a crystal is less personal, and you do not know what you are buying specifically or what condition it will arrive in. So, it is essential when you buy online that you do your research regarding each stone and crystal and decide what you would like to work with before adding it to your shopping cart.

Cleansing Your Crystals

Once you have bought your crystal (or multiple crystals if you decide that you have the budget for it), you need to cleanse them. This way, they can continue to transfer energy effectively and so that you can align, or "program," the crystal to work solely for you, your soul, and your intentions.

A crystal often goes on a long journey before it finds its way to you. It can become corrupted by absorbing negative energies and emotions during this time. This can become less effective in spells and incantations.

Therefore, you must perform the cleansing step before you begin to use your recently acquired crystals in any spells or rituals, and when using them as charms that you keep on yourself, like in your pocket or as part of jewelry.

In addition to cleansing your stones and crystals the first time you get them, you should also practice doing this now and again. There are times when you feel that they need to be re-cleansed or believe that your spells are not as powerful as usual or don't feel right. After a while, stones and crystals become clouded and saturated from use, so it is important to ensure that they remain cleansed to absorb energies and remain effectively tuned to you. Deciding how often you do this falls on your own judgment. Still, I prefer to cleanse mine every month or every other month, depending on how often I am using them.

Below are a few different ways that you can approach cleansing your crystals and preparing them for the next step in the process, which is charging.

Running Water

The simplest way you can cleanse your gemstones is by rinsing them off under running water. Using this specific method, you will be able to purify them of any negative energies and emotions.

You should rinse each gemstone for one minute before you remove them and gently dab them with a linen or paper towel to dry them. You should use this cleansing technique for hard stones, such as a quartz crystal; softer stones like selenite can break easily.

Saltwater

Another easy way to cleanse your gemstones, but one that can take some time compared to just running your crystals underwater, is by immersing them in saltwater. The salt soaks up any negative or unwanted thoughts or energies from the crystals.

You can use fresh saltwater if you live near the sea, or you can make a saltwater solution at home. To make a saltwater solution, you should take a bowl large enough to fit the crystals that you need to cleanse and fill it with water. Next, add in a tablespoon of salt, and then stir the salt into the water.

Then place your crystals into the solution, and allow them to sit for a few hours or until you feel that the crystals are thoroughly cleansed. (You can let them soak for up to 48 hours.) Once they are cleansed, rinse them off, take them out of the water, and gently dab them dry.

This technique also works well for stones that are hard, like amethysts and quartz. You should not use this method on stones that are soft or that will break easily like selenite, or on ones that are porous and have large pits that can easily absorb water. You should also avoid using it on stones that contain metals.

Brown Rice

A way of cleansing your crystals that works well for any type is by placing them into brown rice. Like the saltwater method, this works to absorb any negative or unwanted thoughts or energies from the crystals. This method is a more gentle approach that you can try, which you can control more efficiently when compared to other methods.

To start, place uncooked brown rice into a bowl and submerge your gemstones into the grains. Let them sit for 24 hours. Once the crystals have been cleansed, you should throw out the rice; do not use it again, because the energies from the stones will have passed into the rice grains.

Natural Light

A new day brings new beginnings, and not just for you but for your crystals, too. For this method of cleansing, you should place your stones outside before the sun goes down in the evening. Set them down on the ground if you can or as close to the ground as possible.

You should leave them there throughout the night and then bring them in before 11 o'clock in the morning the next day. When you use this cleansing method, you should keep your gemstones outside for between 10 and 12 hours. After cleansing, you can wipe your crystals off if they got dirty from being on the ground and take them back inside.

By doing this, you will be able to expose your stones to the moonlight's mystical magic and let them soak up the first morning rays. This is an incredible technique that you can use to cleanse and energize your gemstones for the next time you use them.

You can use this cleansing method for most polished stones, but you should avoid doing this with crystals, soft stones, and stones with vibrant colors, as this can cause them to become dull or damaged.

Sage

Sage is a great herb that is used for blessing, healing, and cleansing. You can use it to cleanse the energy in a house when you first move in. Also, suppose there have been some significant changes in your home. You feel that the energies there have become saturated with negativity. In that case, sage can be used to cleanse the area before calling on the spirits for guidance so that bad spirits are not brought into your circle. Additionally, you can sleep with some sage in a pouch under your pillow to rid yourself of nightmares.

There are many other benefits that sage can bring into your life when used. You should explore its properties as you continue your crystal journey and learn new spells. Using sage to smudge your stones and crystals is an excellent way to revert them back to their original state and empower them to become more effective in your magic spells. This method can be used for any type of stone or crystal and is the most effective way to cleanse them.

To smudge your crystals, you should have sage, either loose or bundled, a bowl that will not burn or melt, and some matches. If you have chosen a bundled sage stick, you should hold it at an angle, light it, and then burn for about 20 seconds. Next, blow the flames out gently, leaving only the tips lit with embers while the sage begins to smoke. If you are using loose sage, you should place them inside the bowl and burn them there.

Once the smoke begins to form at the end of the sage, pick up your stone, and hold it in the smoke for 30 seconds. If you have not cleansed your gemstones in a while or feel that it needs to be cleansed for longer, you can continue to smudge it for another 30 seconds. You should repeat this for each of your stones.

Sound

While the previous methods work well and are effective for cleansing your crystals, you might experience problems with using them with all of your stones and crystals once your collection has grown substantially. You may also have issues with the techniques mentioned above if you have invested in powerful geodes for your home, which is also quite heavy. As a solution to this, you can use sound healing to cleanse your stones and crystals on a large scale.

In the area where the stones are located, you should place an object that makes a single sound. You can use something such as a triangle, bell, chanting from yourself, a CD, a music application, or a tuning fork. These will make one continuous sound that your stones and crystals will vibrate with at the same frequency, which resets and cleanses them.

You should play the sound loud enough that your crystals can feel the vibration of it. Let it play for about five to ten minutes or until you feel that your stones and crystals have been cleansed thoroughly. You can use this cleansing method with any stone.

Using a Larger Stone

If you have a few small stones, you can use a larger stone or crystal slab to cleanse them. To do this, you will place your stones on top of the stone or crystal slab and leave them there for 24 hours. The larger stone slab works by letting, the smaller stones and crystals vibrate to the larger stone's same frequency. It balances and synchronizes their energies with the bigger stone, cleansing the gemstones. This cleansing method works well for any stone or crystal.

Using Smaller Stones

When we think about cleansing our stones and crystals, we do not always realize that some stones can cleanse others, such as clear quartz, hematite, and carnelian. To start cleansing your other stones and crystals using these other crystals, you should place them into a bowl, and then put the stone or crystal that you want to cleanse on top of them.

You should leave your stone to cleanse for 24 hours, and then you can remove them from the bowl and put them away. Using this method, you can only restore one stone at a time, so it is a bit slower than other techniques, but it works well to cleanse your stones effectively. You can use this method for any stone.

Breath

While there are many methods that you can use to cleanse your crystals, some are not as well-known as others. By using your breath, you can quickly and effectively cleanse your crystals. The only drawback to using this method is that you need to do one at a time, and it will only work for small gemstones.

To use your breath to cleanse your crystal, you should start by holding the gemstone in the palm of your hand that is more dominant. Next, you should close your eyes and focus on what you want to happen and what outcome you want to achieve from the exercise. In this case, you want to cleanse your stone.

Then, open your eyes and hold the stone up to your face. Next, exhale in short, powerful bursts onto the stone through your nose for 30 seconds. This cleansing method synchronizes your breathing with the stone's vibrations, cleansing it at its highest vibration levels.

Visualization

Another cleansing method many do not know about is visualization. Many feel that this method is the safest when compared to others. Still, not everyone is comfortable or confident enough to use this technique. It can take some time to use visualization for all of your crystals, especially if you have an extensive collection. Still, it is incredibly effective and can be utilized for any stone.

To perform this cleanse, you should start by sitting down in a meditative pose and balancing your emotions and energy. Then, pick up the stone that you want to cleanse and hold it in the palms of your hands. Imagine that a source of energy is coming from your hands and engulfing the stone, becoming brighter and stronger with each passing second. Next, you should visualize any flaws and negative energies surrounding your stone and cleanse these impurities from your hands.

You should continue this visualization for about one minute or until you feel that the stone's energies have been reset and that it has been cleansed.

Programming and Activating Your Crystals

Once you have cleansed your stones and crystals, it is time for you to 'program' or attune the crystal to your soul, emotions, and intentions for using it. You want to give it a purpose to set it out from the rest of your stone and crystal collection. This is an important step that you should perform before using your gemstone in your magic and spells.

Suppose you do not take the time to program your crystals. You will find that the crystal might not focus its energy on a spell you are performing and that you are not experiencing the outcome that you were expecting when you are performing your magic or specific rituals. To ensure that the crystal works for you, your intentions, and your magic, it needs to be individually tuned to you. Otherwise, it will not be effective.

To program your crystal, you should sit down in a meditative state and hold the stone in your hand while you do so. Visualize your intentions and what you want the stone to do for you.

You can also place it on your third eye chakra, which is in the center of your forehead and between your eyebrows. Or on one of your other chakras or areas of your body if you want the stone to activate a specific area or chakra when performing your spells. If you're going to use the stone differently later on, then you can reprogram it after it has been cleansed.

While you are meditating, you should visualize that the energy from the stone is communicating with your soul's energy and emotions and combining it to become one to take care of your goals or possible outcome for the magic spell you are intending to perform. You can visualize this quietly or, if you are comfortable doing so, you can also physically talk to the stone.

Assume this is your first time and you are unsure of what to expect. In that case, you can approach this process by telling your crystal exactly how you are feeling, what spell you are going to perform, or which area of your life or body they should focus on. You should also think about what outcome you are hoping to achieve. By doing this, you can ensure that you and the crystal are working towards the same goal and that there is no miscommunication.

When you feel that your soul and the gem are in sync and ready to work together towards a united goal, you can begin your magic spell. You should always remember to thank your crystal for working with you before you start the spell, as well as after you have finished your spellwork. This will help you and your crystal's energies continue to operate well together.

There may be times when you have already cleansed your crystals, but they still feel saturated, dull, and heavy. When this happens, you will need to consider activating your crystal. The process of activating the crystal lets you provide it with a renewed sense of purpose and energy.

You can activate your crystal, such as using breath work and breathing onto the crystal in a controlled tone to refocus your crystal's energy, talking to it, and singing to it. You can also take your crystal out to a place where it can bathe in the energy of natural surroundings, like a hiking trail, the park, or the beach.

If your stone continues to feel heavy and clouded, even if you have taken it out and tried to activate your crystals, then it is time for a cleanse.

4
ENERGIES

To better understand your crystals, how they work, and what spells they would pair most effectively with when used. You should take some time to understand what type of energy each stone emits - namely, projective energy and receptive energy. By knowing what kind of energy your stone uses, you will be able to communicate better with your crystals. Especially in spell work and daily when cleansing, recharging, activating, and interacting with your crystals.

Projective Stones

Projective stones are powerful and filled with dynamic energy used to amplify a stone's healing, protection, courage, luck, success, and divination. Projective stones are often used to cast their energies out into the world. They are often utilized in spells that are dedicated to helping other people. They are also great for performing spells that benefit your mind, body, and spirit physically, such as promoting self-healing and self-confidence.

Projective stones are tied to the sun and the planets Mars, Mercury, and Uranus. They are associated with the fire and air elements. As such, these stones possess great power to heal, provide protection, make you feel more courageous, increase your energy, and improve your vitality.

These will feel heavier in your hands when compared to receptive stones, and when you handle them, you might get the feeling that there is an energy charge being released. Because projective stones always feel like they are charged, you do not have to spend long in the charging and activating phase. You just need to make them aware of your intentions. They are always ready to be used in your daily life and spell work as they are needed.

Because these stones are associated with the fire and air elements. They are often found to be dark or vibrant, brightly colored stones, such as gold, orange, red, and yellow. However, there are some clear, see-through crystals considered to be projective stones, such as clear quartz.

The following stones are projective:

Amber	Apache Tear	Asbestos	Aventurine
Banded Agate	Black Agate	Bloodstone	Brown Agate
Carnelian	Cat's Eye	Chiastolite	Citrine
Cross Stone	Diamond	Flint	Fluorite
Garnet	Hematite	Herkimer Quartz	Lava
Mica	Mottled Jasper	Obsidian	Onyx
Opal	Orange Calcite	Pipestone	Pumice
Red Agate	Red Jasper	Red Tourmaline	Rhodochrosite
Rhodonite	Ruby	Rutilated Quartz	Sard
Sardonyx	Serpentine	Sphene	Spinel
Sunstone	Tiger's Eye	Topaz	Tourmalated Quartz
Zircon			

Receptive Stones

Receptive stones are just as powerful as projective stones. However, where projective stones are filled with dynamic energy, receptive stones bring a calming, serene static energy into your life. These stones are focused on helping you on a spiritual level, and they fill you up with warm, soothing energy.

Receptive stones are tied to the moon and the planets Jupiter, Neptune, Saturn, and Venus. They are associated with the Earth and water elements. As a result, these stones provide spiritual and emotional benefits to you. When using receptive stones, the spells that you cast should be focused on uplifting you and healing you in a powerful and calming way in mind, body, and spirit.

Because these stones remove many negative energies and emotions from ourselves and the environment around us, they can become saturated and dull quickly. When this happens, you should cleanse your crystal so that it continues to work effectively in your magic practices.

The receptive stones are associated with the Earth and water elements and, as such, are found in various natural colors, such as blue, green, pink, and purple, and more neutral colors like black, white, and silver. As well as these beautiful, soothing colors, some receptive stones have facets that shift to different colors when the light reflects off of them. There are also semi-transparent receptive stones.

The following stones are receptive:

Alum	Amethyst	Aquamarine	Azurite
Beryl	Black Tourmaline	Blue Calcite	Blue Lace Agate
Blue Quartz	Blue Tourmaline	Brown Jasper	Celestite
Chalcedony	Chalcedony	Chrysocolla	Chrysoprase
Coal	Coral	Cross Stone	Emerald
Fossils	Geodes	Green Agate	Green Calcite
Green Jasper	Green Quartz	Green Tourmaline	Holey Stones
Jade	Jet	Kunzite	Lapis Lazuli
Malachite	Marble	Moonstone	Moss Agate
Mother-Of-Pearl	Olivine	Opal	Pearl
Peridot	Petrified Wood	Pink Calcite	Pink Tourmaline
Quartz Crystal	Rose Quartz	Salt	Sapphire
Selenite	Sodalite	Smokey Quartz	Turquoise

Exceptions

There are times when a stone has both projective energies and receptive energies. So it becomes difficult to classify it accurately as one kind or the other. When this happens, you should take some time to meditate and communicate with your crystal.

Most of the time, you will need to rely on your own experiences to decide if a crystal is one variety or the other based on the different energies you have encountered with other crystals that were projective or receptive.

What is terrific about the types of crystals that have properties of both energies is that they are often molded into having a particular energy type or specific properties from both energy types, depending on how you have decided to use it.

Therefore, if you mostly use the crystal to cast spells to heal and protect other people, it will become projective. If you cast spells to heal and improve yourself, then it will become receptive.

Some examples of crystals that have exceptions and can be either projective or receptive include amethyst, basic quartz crystal, cross-stone, and opal.

5
CRYSTALS TO USE IN MAGIC

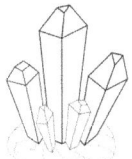

There are hundreds of different varieties of crystals in the world. Ranging from common gemstones that can be found in any occult shop like basic quartz or amethyst, to ones that are even rarer than diamonds. Each gemstone has its own color, unique internal structure, properties, and uses.

Below, I have provided information on thirteen of the most popular crystals commonly used in magic. These include basic quartz, rose quartz, amethyst, citrine, moonstone, carnelian, bloodstone, jade, lapis lazuli, malachite, tiger's eye, jet, and hematite.

Basic Quartz

Basic quartz, also known as clear quartz, is a colorless, mostly transparent crystal. If you have one in its uncut and unpolished form, it could appear to be a cloudy white color or frosted. Some are then cut and polished from this state and often retain a somewhat frosted appearance. You would find basic quartz in nature in a pillar shape or a pointed cluster.

Basic quartz is one of the most common crystals that people buy from occult stores and when shopping online when they start their crystal collection. This is mainly due to its properties and abilities to cleanse other crystals. Basic quartz is found in abundance on Earth.

This crystal is used in various ways today, such as in electronic circuits, microphones, watches, and computer chips. It is no longer only utilized as it once was in jewelry, healing, and magical practices like it had been in the past. This is because the quartz crystal is well-balanced and operates at a specific frequency that helps to maintain a watch's movements to keep time. It is also able to produce and sustain an electric charge.

The ancient Greeks gave basic quartz the name "krystallos," which means "ice crystal." They believed that these crystals were pieces of eternally-frozen ice because of their clarity and transparency. Since this stone is in such abundance on Earth, most ancient cultures have their own experiences, histories, and mythologies tied to this crystal. Thus, they have given the crystal different properties throughout history.

This crystal is well-known for its healing properties. Due to its shape, it can effectively soak up any negative energy and emotions, as well as store and release them. Because of this specific quality of quartz, it can be used to protect against and reduce the effects made to your mind, body, and spirit by radiation and electromagnetic energies.

If you are experiencing a chakra block and do not feel like yourself, you can use this crystal to rebalance your energies and remove the block. With basic quartz, you can improve any health condition that you or someone you know is suffering from. It can also be used to boost your immune system and overall health.

Quartz is often utilized in various ways in holistic healing practices, such as in acupuncture. In ancient China, acupuncturists would apply this crystal to their needles' tips to help improve treatment and recovery. This use, as well as many others, is still seen today in modern times.

Basic quartz crystal can also amplify energy. Thus, it is often used to cleanse and program other crystals and increase the effectiveness of magic and spells. You can use a single quartz slab or multiple smaller quartz crystals to cleanse your other stones and crystals.

These cleansing methods are very useful because of the quartz crystal's ability to soak up, store, and remove any negative energy from the stone. Using a quartz crystal will allow other stones to vibrate at the same frequency, completely resetting them.

Rose Quartz

Rose quartz crystal is a light rose pink color that is usually transparent. It is similar to a quartz crystal, but it also often appears to be a milky, solid color. You will often find rose quartz cut and polished into a tumbled or round sphere shape, but you can also find it in its raw, uncut state.

This crystal is not as common as basic quartz, but it is still one of the most natural crystals to find. It comes from Brazil, India, Japan, Madagascar, South Africa, and the United States. In contrast, basic quartz is found all across the world.

The first use of rose quartz crystals was jewelry. This use dates back to the times of ancient Mesopotamia in 7000 BCE. Then it was later utilized by the Assyrians around 800 to 600 BCE, and then the Romans. Ancient civilizations like Egypt, Rome, and Greece used rose quartz as talismans.

The Egyptians believed that by placing rose quartz in their jewelry and using them as talismans, that they could stop themselves from aging. Meanwhile, in ancient Rome, people created seals from rose quartz that would signify a person's position, status, or family crest. They would use these seals to stamp hot wax to seal their letters and other important documents.

Later on, in the Middle Ages, people used rose quartz in healing and would grind up the crystal for healing potions and tonics. Rose quartz was after that used in the Americas in amulets to help improve mood and stabilize emotions, ridding people of negative emotions like anger and disappointment.

In modern times, rose quartz crystal is known as the stone of love. It helps the person who uses or wears the crystal to become more open to receiving love and loving others. This stone also has calming energies that can help balance your mind, body, and spirit. Intending to enable you to let go of past emotions that you have been unable to release.

If you are looking for a partner or are struggling to meet someone, you can use rose quartz and cast a spell to bring positive and healthy relationships. If you have already met someone you like, but you are unable to talk to them and tell them how you feel, using rose quartz can help you gain more confidence in life and have a much-needed heart-to-heart with them.

Meanwhile, if you are married and are not finding time to be intimate with your partner or have some issues, you can place rose quartz underneath your pillow. This will help you resolve your conflicts with your partner and influence your relationship to become more sexual. It might even assist you in becoming more confident in trying new things in the bedroom.

Suppose you are struggling to come to terms with the loss of someone you were close to. In that case, you can use rose quartz to rebalance your positive emotions and remove the negative ones. So that you can come to terms with what has happened and what is happening now in your life. Rose quartz will help you heal your heart so that you can refocus on the present and get past difficult times.

If you feel anxious or stressed, you can also look to rose quartz to provide you with a sense of calm and help reduce your stress, releasing any tension you are holding onto. Rose quartz is a soothing gem. You should turn to this stunning crystal whenever you do not feel like yourself for the healing and peacefulness that your body, mind, and soul needs.

Amethyst

Amethyst is purple/lavender colored and transparent. It has sharp, pointed crystals that form in clusters in its raw or geode forms. You can often find amethysts as a single, thin crystal with a pointed tip, a stunning geode, or a cluster. Using an amethyst geode in your home or as a centerpiece in your healing corner has become popular in modern times because of how beautiful it looks in this form.

This powerful gem is one of the most abundant and commonly used crystals available, along with basic quartz. It is easy to find when buying from an occult shop or online. The amethyst crystal comes from Brazil, Great Britain, Canada, East Africa, India, Mexico, Russia, Siberia, Sri Lanka, the United States, and Uruguay.

The people of ancient Greece believed that by wearing amethysts on their bodies or in their jewelry and embellishing their mugs and chalices with amethysts (or crafting them from the crystals), they could reduce their chance of becoming drunk. They believed they would have a higher alcohol tolerance and would be able to drink more wine and alcohol before feeling intoxicated.

Later, in the Middle Ages, amethysts were used as talismans worn by soldiers who went off to battle. They believed that amethyst could provide them with protection and heal them or help them recover faster if injured on the battlefield.

It was also thought that the crystal could result in having a clearer head when a soldier needed to make decisions. It also was believed to improve one's understanding of what needed to be done.

The British have been known to wear jewelry and crowns with precious stones and crystals embedded in them. They considered amethysts to be very valuable. They would use these stones decoratively along with emeralds, rubies, and sapphires, which were of similar value.

The British royal family would wear amethysts to signify their power and status. They would also use them in ceremonies such as coronations. These traditions are still observed today. Religious officials like bishops are also known to wear amethysts in their rings.

Suppose you are not feeling like yourself or think that your judgment is clouded or that you have been struggling to make crucial decisions. In that case, you can use an amethyst talisman or spell to help you refocus on your goal and what it is that you want. With the amethyst crystal, you will be able to view things from a new perspective, increase your creativity, and make better decisions.

Amethyst can also be used for protection and protect you against people who talk behind your back or wish you ill. This crystal also works on a spiritual level, protecting you from psychic attacks. Amethyst does this by expelling negative energies and replacing them with the crystal's positive energy.

Similar to how it was utilized in the ancient Greeks' times; the amethyst crystal is used to help rid someone of addictive behaviors, such as obsessive-compulsive disorder (OCD), as well as food, drug, smoking, and alcohol addictions. By wearing or using an amethyst crystal in magic, you can successfully free yourself and your mind of these addictions.

You can also perform a detoxifying spell to help you detox from these addictions and increase the rate at which your body heals and recovers when cutting the habits from your life. If you have an addiction to gambling, this crystal can also ensure that you become more frugal with the ways you are spending your money. This helps you break free of the habit so that you can start doing something productive with the money you would otherwise use gambling.

When utilized in the home, the amethyst crystal provides healing and calming properties to you and your family. Suppose your children are stressing about an upcoming exam. In that case, you can place a charged amethyst crystal in their bedroom or in the room that they use to study to reduce their stress and soak up information more effectively.

If you or someone in your family are having trouble sleeping, you can place amethyst under their pillow. This will help you or your loved one have more peaceful dreams, and it should curb any nightmares you or they might have been previously having. Amethyst can also help improve insomnia so you can fall asleep more quickly and stop waking up multiple times in the night.

Amethyst is used as the birthstone for the Pisces zodiac sign. However, it also provides benefits when used by other zodiac signs, such as Scorpio and Aquarius. If you are a Pisces, amethyst can be used for its calming and tranquil qualities to help you relax and unwind.

This crystal is perfect for stabilizing your mind, body, and spirit if you are an Aquarius. A Scorpio is creative, passionate, and full of emotion, and sometimes their feelings can get the best of them. Using amethyst, a Scorpio can stabilize their emotions and become able to approach things with a clear head. If you are a Scorpio, utilize amethyst to give yourself the calming energy that you need to put your mind at ease.

Citrine

A citrine is a yellow to yellow-orange or yellow-brown stone. It is transparent and has sharp pointed crystals that form in clusters in its raw or geode forms, similar to amethyst. You can find citrine as a single, thin crystal with a pointed tip, as a geode, or in a cluster. This crystal is often cut and polished into a gemstone that is set into a decorative ring.

Citrine is rarer and not as widely available as the other crystals that have already been mentioned. Frequently, you will find that shops are not selling real citrine crystals, and that it is, in fact, amethyst crystals that have been heat-treated to look like citrine. This is easy to do because of similarities in the structure that the two crystals share.

When you buy a citrine crystal, you should ensure that you are buying citrine and not a knock-off. Otherwise, your citrine crystal will not function as intended. In case that the shop's citrine crystals are selling at similar prices to amethysts, this might be a good indication that they are not selling real citrine.

You can also tell the difference between natural citrine and heat-treated citrine by having a good look at the crystal. If the crystal has any hints of purple or has a burned-in yellow-brown look on the tips of the crystal or cluster, it is probably heat-treated. Natural citrine has a more substantial, yellow-orange to smoky yellow-brown color along the entirety of the crystal or stone.

The citrine crystal comes from Brazil, Great Britain, France, Madagascar, Russia, and the United States.

Citrine is a popular gemstone that has been used in jewelry throughout history. The gemstone was first used decoratively by the people of ancient Greece between 300 and 150 BCE.

Later, in the Middle Ages, the Celts and the Scots used citrine in their jewelry and amulets to provide protection against illness and injury, to help keep their skin clear if they struggled with acne or other skin conditions, and to rid themselves of inappropriate or destructive thoughts. Besides these health benefits that the gemstone provided, you would find many Scottish men adorning their sword hilts and daggers decoratively with the crystal.

Citrine is known as the stone of success and wealth. By using this crystal in your spellwork or wearing it as jewelry or as a charm on your body, you will be able to increase your wealth and success in everyday life and possible business ventures.

The citrine crystal helps you think more clearly and make important decisions, which, in turn, draws wealth to you or your business or can bring you success in daily life. The crystal also helps you become stricter with how you spend your money and your time, ensuring that you retain your wealth and success.

There are times when we hit a slump. We might feel like we are not enough or do not have enough confidence to get something done. If you are feeling like this, you can use a citrine crystal to help lift your mood. You can perform spells or create talismans to help you become more courageous and increase your self-confidence and self-respect.

Similarly to the amethyst, using citrine can help you overcome addictions and finally break any bad habits you have picked up throughout your life. This crystal can also heal you of any underlying reasons you picked up the addiction or bad habit in the first place. Additionally, it can provide you with a sense of hope and support while you break away from those addictions.

If you are trying to choose between amethyst and citrine for breaking an addiction or bad habit, I would suggest that you choose a citrine crystal. When you are healing your body of these habits, the energies that the crystals absorb can cause them to become saturated and heavy very quickly. Citrine is preferred because it does not hold onto any negative or destructive energy that it absorbs. It can cleanse itself without the use of various cleansing methods.

Citrine is used as the birthstone for the Sagittarius zodiac sign. It also provides benefits when used by other zodiac signs, such as Aries, Libra, and Scorpio. If you are a Sagittarius, you know that you are always looking for new adventures and things to try. Citrine can help ground you and ensure that you remain true to yourself and your beliefs, no matter where life takes you.

An Aries is ambitious, passionate, and confident. Using citrine either as a charm or in their spellwork, they can make their dreams come to fruition. Using this crystal can make you more optimistic about life and the future if you are a Libra. It can also provide you with the balance that you naturally need in life. A Scorpio has their ups and downs, and when they become angry, depressed, or lonely, their emotions can become amplified. When this happens, they can use a citrine crystal to help pick them up and remove these negative emotions.

Moonstone

The moonstone is a crystal that comes in various colors, such as blue, cream, green, white, and yellow. It is usually seen with a combination of these different colors like, for example, cream with white stripes or mostly blue with a few cream highlights. You can find the moonstone in its raw, natural shape or cut and polished into tumbled gemstones.

The moonstone is a very commonly found and used stone. Thus, it can be obtained easily through any occult shop or online. It originates in Australia, India, and Sri Lanka. These stones are often cut into various shapes and sizes to be used in rings, necklaces, and other jewelry. They are quite popular, especially in their white and cream forms.

The moonstone was first known to be utilized by the ancient Indians and in Hindu mythology. The Hindu god Ganesh was depicted with a moonstone embedded on his forehead covering his third eye chakra. The Indian people believed that the moonstone provided the person who was using or wearing it with divination powers and allowed them to tell prophecies of the future. They also found that by placing the moonstone inside your mouth, you would receive powers of wisdom.

Because of the color of the moonstone and how it reflects light, the ancient Romans believed that the stone was created from the moonlight. The Romans thought that Diana, the goddess of the moon, was depicted in the moonstone. Thus, this gemstone was well-favored.

The Romans also believed that the moonstone brought about desire and attraction towards another person. They thought that when two people wore the moonstone and met under the moonlight's peak, they would fall in love with each other. The moonstone is also known to be a protective stone and would provide travelers with safety that crossed the sea by the moon's light.

Later, in ancient Eastern Asian cultures, it was believed that the moonstone brought good luck to the person using it. They also thought if they had trouble sleeping or trying to fall asleep, the stone would help them do these things more efficiently and rid them of any bad dreams or worry that might keep them up at night.

They also believed that the light reflecting off the moonstone portrayed a living spirit inside the stone, similar to the Romans.

In Asian culture, the number thirteen was unlucky. So couples would receive a moonstone on their thirteenth wedding anniversary to bring them good luck. Every thirteen years, the stone's energy would help to drive away negative energies that might be caused in the relationship due to the association of the number thirteen.

When you have made some choices that have not panned out as expected, you will benefit from using a moonstone to help you see the decisions you have made with more clarity. It can also help you develop your intuition so that the next time you make a decision, you are more informed, and your intuition is improved.

Have you had experience with the spiritual world, or have you had a few psychic moments or déjà vu recently. Would you like to better develop your skills to improve your psychic abilities? Or, do you wish to try and communicate with someone who has been trying to contact you? If so, you can wear a moonstone bracelet or necklace to increase your spiritual connection and become more clairvoyant.

The moonstone has also been known to have a calming effect on a person. It can stabilize your energies and emotions. It is often used to help reduce stress and allow you to keep your cool during occurrences that might set you on edge or cause you to overreact.

Along with all the other benefits, the moonstone provides the wearer with positive effects such as improved digestion, increased fertility and likelihood to conceive, reduced premenstrual symptoms, protection during pregnancy, and removal of toxins from your body, and improved sleep at night if you have insomnia.

Carnelian

Carnelian is a translucent stone found in a variety of colors, like brown, orange, pink, and red. This gemstone is cut down from one larger rock into several smaller stones. These stones are mostly bought in their tumbled, polished form, but they can also be found in their rough, raw stone form.

Carnelian is another common gemstone, and it is easy to find when buying from an occult store or online. The carnelian stone comes from Great Britain, the Czech Republic, India, Ireland, Peru, Romania, and Slovakia.

The carnelian stone is also identified as the stone of luck. In ancient Egypt, it was used by the goddess Isis to provide protection to the dead as they passed over to the other side. The Egyptians believed that by using and wearing this stone when you were buried, you would pass through the gates of the afterlife more easily.

Similarly to the ancient Egyptians using rose quartz, the ancient Romans made seals from carnelian stone. Carnelians would also be used to making jewelry such as rings, earrings, and necklaces, and they were often carved into the shape of an animal.

These jewelry pieces would be worn to provide the wearer with good luck, protection, and courage. The ancient Romans, as well as the ancient Greeks before them, would embed carnelian into their signet rings for similar reasons and display that they were important.

Carnelian is another stone that you can use to cleanse other stones in your collection. By utilizing a large carnelian slab and placing other stones and crystals on top of it, or using multiple carnelian stones in a bowl and placing the stone that you want to cleanse on top, you can remove any bad energy surrounding the stones and crystals, cleansing them effectively.

In ancient Egypt, this stone was once used when the Egyptian dead were buried to help them cross over to the afterlife. Similarly, the carnelian stone can ease your mind and help you accept the thought of death if you or a loved one is suffering from a terminal illness or has recently passed.

It also helps you make decisions and improves your perception while you are still alive, allowing you to make choices with a clear mind. It also helps to improve the decisions that you make regarding your lifestyle, and it increases your ability to become successful.

Suppose you feel that you are overwhelmed by life and are often in your own world and no longer noticing the things that are happening around you. In that case, you can use the carnelian to help you to focus on what is happening at the moment. Using this stone, you can increase your perception of the world around you and remove any strenuous exhaustion that you feel could be the reason for your loss of focus. This stone will remove these negative emotions and energy and replace them with positive emotions that can help you enjoy your life and the things happening around you more.

The carnelian stone has many health benefits, too. These include improving your fertility and ability to conceive, increasing your flexibility and mood, healing your aches and pains, removing any pain from arthritis, and helping you combat depression. This stone also works well to remove toxins from your kidneys, improve their function, heal broken bones and ligaments, and increase the movement of blood around your body and to your organs.

Carnelian is used as the birthstone for the Virgo zodiac sign. It also provides benefits when used by zodiac signs such as Aries, Taurus, Gemini, and Leo. A Virgo works hard but can worry and are too strict with themselves and others. Using a carnelian can help display a Virgo's passion and motivation in both their profession and relationships. This can help them refocus on what goals they want in life. When people see how motivated and passionate they can be, it can help pave the path for them to become more successful.

Suppose an Aries is feeling uncertain about something or about themselves. In that case, they can use the carnelian stone to help them see things with more clarity so that they can make a decision more easily. If a Taurus finds themselves in a situation where they feel that they have no control, the carnelian stone can help them find a way out of the situation.

A Gemini is a naturally energized and happy star sign. Using the carnelian stone, you can amplify these traits in you and become more motivated to reach for your goals. Leo is enthusiastic about their dreams and passionate about life. The carnelian stone can help them become more creative and assist them in achieving their goals, similarly to a Gemini. This stone can also bring out the natural leadership qualities of a Leo.

Bloodstone

The bloodstone is a green-colored stone that has hints of red or yellow jasper in it. You will commonly find this stone in a green and red color combination, with a green and yellow color combination being seen less frequently. Bloodstone is a tumbled, polished stone, but it can also be bought in its rough, raw stone form. There are two different types of bloodstone: heliotrope, which appears to be transparent and has spots of red or yellow jasper splattered across it, and plasma, which varies from translucent to opaque with hardly any spots.

This stone is not as common as others mentioned previously. However, it is still reasonably easy to find when buying from an occult shop or online. The bloodstone comes from Australia, Brazil, China, the Czech Republic, India, and Russia.

The ancient Greeks used to call this stone "heliotrope." In Greek, this word meant "to turn the sun." The Greeks believed that when the stone was placed in water, the sun would become red, turning the sky red. The name "bloodstone" was only given to the stone later on when used in religious events and ceremonies. It was believed to signify the blood of Christ.

The bloodstone is a beautiful healing stone that removes negative energy from your body and improves your immune system, allowing you to fight infections and viruses more easily. This stone also helps to boost your metabolism and open blockages so that your blood can flow through your body more efficiently. True to its name, the bloodstone helps remove toxins and improves blood-related health conditions, such as leukemia.

When you use the bloodstone, it can provide you with courageous energy to feel more optimistic, and like you can conquer anything you set your heart to. The bloodstone can also help you become more aware of your surroundings, allowing you to avoid situations that make you feel uncomfortable or unsafe. This stone also helps to remove any feelings of confusion and self-doubt, enabling you to make a decision on something more quickly.

Let's say you feel that you are in a bad mood. You're experiencing difficult times that cause you to lash out at others and become more irritated and impatient in certain circumstances. You can use the bloodstone to surround yourself with spiritual calming energies. This way, you can handle certain situations in a better way. It will also help you be more patient and understanding towards other people.

Bloodstone is used as the birthstone for the Aries zodiac sign. If you are an Aries, this stone helps amplify your positive characteristics. It increases your confidence and belief in yourself and improves your leadership qualities. It gives you the strength and courage to face anything that comes your way.

Jade

The jade crystal is usually green in color. It can appear to be either translucent or have a solid creamy look. While we think of the jade crystal as being green, it actually comes in many other colors. These are unsuspecting colors such as brown, blue, cream, lavender, orange, red, white, yellow, and a mixture of green and blue. You will mostly find this crystal in its tumbled form or cut and polished into a disc, sometimes with a hole made in the center. However, you will be able to find jade in its rough, raw stone form as well.

There are two different types of jade, namely nephrite jade and jadeite jade. Nephrite jade is found in green and white colors, with the whiter shades being well-favored and rare to find. Nephrite jade is a more hardened stone compared to jadeite jade, and it is paler in color and not as vibrant. The green color of the nephrite jade is quite darkly pigmented, and the stone does not have much shine to it. Comparatively, jadeite jade comes in a variety of bright colors and can range from translucent to relatively transparent.

Nephrite jade crystals are more commonly found, while jadeite jade is rarer and are also more expensive to obtain. Because nephrite jade is more commonly found, you can find these easily in an occult shop or online. In contrast, you might not find jadeite jade as effortlessly. The jade stone comes from China, Italy, the Middle East, Myanmar, Russia, and the United States.

Jade originated in Central America and was used by the Aztecs and the Mayans. They would embed jadeite jade into their decorative ornaments, jewelry, and religious artifacts. They would also use it for its healing properties and in medicine. Meanwhile, the early Spanish civilization used jade to reduce their pain. They would achieve this by holding the crystal against the side of their body where it hurt until the aches and pains went away.

The most popular use of the jade crystal was seen in ancient China. The Chinese would carve symbolic shapes and depictions into nephrite and jadeite jade stones. The image carved into the stone would provide the person who was using or working with the jade with the depiction's properties. For example, if they carved a butterfly into the jade, it would allow them to lead a long life.

They would also use this stone to create jewelry pieces, such as pins, necklaces, and earrings, and they would set them into a metal frame in the shapes of these motifs. Popular designs the Chinese used included bats, butterflies, dragons, peace signs, and a bi, which is a disc with a hole made in the center.

Using the jade crystal, you can balance your energies and emotions, synchronizing what you feel in your heart with what you know to be true in your mind. In this way, you can come to understand yourself better and even learn new things about yourself. The jade crystal also helps to remove negative energies and thoughts from your mind. It can replace them with a calming, balancing energy so that you can be more carefree and make better decisions by improving your intuition.

The jade stone is well-known for its cleansing properties. As such, it can be used to cleanse the toxins' body and help your body better filter your blood and other nutrients that are carried in and around your body. This makes the jade stone an excellent choice to help improve the functioning of your kidneys. This, in turn, helps reduce the effects of kidney infection and kidney failure.

The jade stone also offers other health benefits to the person wearing or using the stone, such as helping heal open wounds and injuries that do not seem to be healing. It also helps to improve the rate at which your stitches heal. Additionally, several people use this stone to improve their fertility, which allows them to conceive.

Lapis Lazuli

The lapis lazuli is a semi-opaque blue rock with flecks or veins of gold that envelope the crystal. You will often find it in its raw and unpolished stone form, but sometimes you can find it tumbled and polished.

While the lapis lazuli can be obtained easily from any occult shop or online, this stone can be quite expensive. I do not suggest that you buy it right off the bat after starting your crystal collection (that is unless you need this stone specifically for a spell). The lapis lazuli comes from Afghanistan, Chile, Egypt, Italy, the Middle East, Russia, and the United States.

It is believed that the lapis lazuli has been used by humans for more than 6,500 years, being utilized first by the world's ancient civilizations. This crystal was well-favored by the Sumerians, Egyptians, Chinese, Greeks, and the Romans. They used this crystal because it bore a resemblance to other valued blue crystals, like sapphire and turquoise. These ancient civilizations would use lapis lazuli in amulets, carvings, and jewelry.

The ancient Egyptians would embed lapis lazuli in their statues that depicted their pharaohs and gods. They would also place this gemstone into the masks of the people who were dead to protect them as they crossed over into the afterlife. The Egyptians and the Sumerians in Mesopotamia before them would forge cylinder seals out of lapis lazuli. They would then carve depictions of events and religious ceremonies onto them that were rolled over wet clay to make an impression.

In the Middle Ages and during the Renaissance, many people of a higher class were fascinated by the intense blue color of the lapis lazuli crystal. They would grind it up and use it in their colors to create more vibrant, pigmented blues in their paintings.

The lapis lazuli has been known to provide the wearer or the person using the crystal with divination and intuition. This crystal can open your third eye chakra, improving your connection with the spiritual realm, and improving your psychic abilities. This stone also stabilizes your throat chakra. This allows you to enhance your communication abilities, both with the people around you and the spirits.

The lapis lazuli also provides a person with protection and removes negative, dark energies that might be surrounding you. Let's say someone has been speaking badly about you or wishing ill on you. This stone can protect you against such attacks and cleanse you of any curse or spiritual attack that has been used against you.

The lapis lazuli is also known to be able to amplify your thoughts. Say you are performing a spell, and you do not feel that it is meeting the person that it is directed towards. You could use a lapis lazuli in your spell to enhance the power of your other stone.

It also works to help guide you towards the correct path. It does so by helping you see things more clearly and with a fresh perspective to formulate your own opinions on decisions you are faced with.

The lapis lazuli can also be used for its health benefits. It can help reduce any pain you are feeling and balancing the different energies that course through your body. As a consequence improving depression, strengthening your immune system against infection, and viruses and stabilizing your blood pressure. It can also help to reduce dizziness. Also, by placing a lapis lazuli underneath your pillow, you may be able to sleep better at night.

Malachite

Malachite often has varying patterns of different colors of green and aquamarine-green in its design. In its raw form, this stone can appear to be solid, porous, or foamy. You will often find malachite in its tumbled form, shaped into an oval or other shape and polished, or you can find it in its raw form.

You should be careful when using malachite because it's toxic when handled in its raw form or ground down into a powder. Thus, you should only use malachite in its tumbled and polished forms. There is an exception to this rule if you are experienced working with it or working on a spell or charm with someone who has had experience working and healing with the stone.

Malachite is a less common crystal than previous ones that have been mentioned. Still, they are easy to find when buying from an occult shop or online. Malachite comes from Romania, the Democratic Republic of the Congo, the Middle East, Russia, and Zambia.

The earliest use of malachite was found to be in ancient Israel over 3,000 years ago. The ancient Egyptians used to ground up malachite into a powder and use it in their makeup. Many cultures continued to use it in makeup and as green pigment until the 1800s, when they found that malachite was a toxic substance in its raw and powdered forms. The ancient Egyptians also used this stone in their jewelry and amulets. They would embed it into the headpieces of the pharaohs as decoration.

The stone continued to be used decoratively; the ancient Greeks and the Romans would utilize it to create beautiful sculptures, vases, and other decorative ornaments. Later, the Russians also used the stone in this manner. They actually took it one step further and made larger structures with the stones. Examples include the columns, fireplaces, and other decorative ornaments found in the Malachite Room of the Winter Palace.

Malachite has been used for protection by various different cultures for centuries. The malachite works by soaking up any negative energies and emotions surrounding a person, or any toxins, radiation, or pollutants in the atmosphere around them. It cleanses these emotions and replaces them with positive, healing energies.

This stone can amplify both the positive and the negative energies inside you. Around you, so you must cleanse your crystal before you use it. Make sure to speak good intentions to ensure that your crystal boosts the positive energy and removes the negative energies. This stone should be cleansed after you use it in a spell to purify and cleanse it of the negative energies it may have taken in.

Malachite is especially beneficial when used as a healing stone for women. It provides relief from cramps and helps to relieve pain and make things easier when a woman is giving birth. Additionally, if a person has caught a sexual disease, it can help manage and treat it. This stone also provides other health benefits, such as improving the immune system. It can stabilize blood pressure, improve asthma, heal fractures, reduce inflammation in the joints, cause arthritis and other joint pain, and manage tumors and other growths.

Tiger's Eye

As its name suggests, the tiger's eye has the colors and patterns that one would associate with that of the eye of a tiger. The stone can be found in various colors, such as blue, brown, brown-yellow, pink, and red, with varying patterns on the surface. You can often find a tiger's eye stone in its rough, raw form or tumbled.

The tiger's eye is a relatively rare stone, but it can be easy to find when buying from an occult shop or online. The tiger's eye comes from Australia, India, Mexico, South Africa, and the United States.

This stone is relatively new when compared to others that have been used since the Stone Age. The tiger's eye was first found in South Africa in the 1800s. Because it was considered rare at first, the African tribal leaders and their families would use them in their cultural ceremonies. However, this stone became more frequent and widely used when other mines were found to have this rock in abundance.

The tiger's eye provides the wearer or the person using the stone with protection against people who wish them harm and from curses that have been bound on them by other people. The tiger's eye is often used as a charm or talisman that protects the wearer or the person carrying it from these negative energies. It is believed to dissolve any curses that have been made against them.

When the tiger's eye was first uncovered in South Africa, it was worn on the Zulu warrior's wardress, Shaka Zulu. Because of this, the stone became known as a symbol of great strength. The tiger's eye provides the wearer with the courage and strength to face what comes their way and helps ground them so that they have the confidence to make crucial decisions.

The tiger's eye can help you open your eyes to misconceptions between what you want and what you need. When you use the tiger's eye in magic or wear or carry it with you, it can help you readjust your way of thinking so that you have a better understanding of the essential things in your life. In this way, the stone ensures that you put these values before anything else. This stone can also help you understand the difference between something you think you need and what you actually need in life.

The tiger's eye provides a plethora of health benefits to the person using it. For example, this stone can help you stabilize your body's energies, making you feel more energetic and happy, thereby reducing depression. As the name implies, if you are having difficulties seeing poorly lit areas or at night, you will notice your vision improving and better see in the dark. The tiger's eye also helps mend wounds and broken bones.

Jet

A jet stone is a dense, black-colored rock that often has a brown sheen on its surface. This stone is made from wood that has become fossilized. It does not have much of a shine in its raw form and looks strikingly similar to coal. You can find this stone in its tumbled form, cut and polished into a specific shape like an oval or circular disk, or in its rough, raw form.

This gemstone is commonly used and is easy to find when buying from an occult shop or online. The jet stone does not come from just one place but can be found all over the world.

This stone was first used in ancient Egypt and amongst the Pueblo Indian tribe in the Southwestern United States. The Egyptians and the Pueblo people would bury this stone with their dead to provide them with protection when they crossed over into the afterlife.

The ancient Romans were the first civilization to use the jet stone for decorative purposes and for its magical abilities. Later, in 1500 BCE, the English also used this stone decoratively and in their jewelry. During the Victorian Era, it became popular as the stone of mourning. People would wear it when they were grieving the departed.

When someone wears or uses the jet stone, it can form a bond with that individual. It will often only respond when the person who uses the stone is communicating with it. If you purchase the stone from a store or inherit a jet stone from a friend or family member, then you should ensure that you cleanse the stone before you use it, since it can become fixed to a single person. The jet stone also absorbs energies when used in magic and will need to be cleansed after each time you use it in a spell.

When you use or wear a jet stone, it can improve your psychic abilities and open you to new spiritual and psychic encounters. It can stabilize your emotions and energies, resulting in a decrease in depression. It can bring emotional balance into your life.

The jet stone is also often used in spells to help you become wealthier and better handle your money. The jet stone does this by helping you see with clarity where you might manage your money in the wrong way. It also provides you with a sense of balance that you need to become more financially stable. If you cast a charm on the crystal, you can place it inside a box of money or in a safe where you keep your money.

Hematite

Hematite is a black, red, or silver-colored rock that is made from iron oxide. The iron oxide in this rock often gives it a mixed red-brown, rust-like appearance. You can usually find hematite in its tumbled form or cut and polished into the shape of an oval disc. Other ways you can find this crystal are in its raw rock and crystalline forms.

Its colors can appear to be quite dull when it is in its raw form, and the rock does not have a polished look to it. However, when it has been polished, it becomes shiny. Hematite is a commonly used crystal and easy to find when buying from an occult shop or online. Hematite comes from Brazil, Britain, Canada, Italy, Sweden, and Switzerland.

This stone has been around for thousands of years. In fact, the first known use of hematite was in the Stone Age, over 164,000 years ago, by a man who has been named the "Pinnacle Point man." He lived in what is known today as South Africa. He would grind up the hematite stone and use it to draw images on the caves' walls where he lived.

Later on, in history, hematite was used by the ancient Egyptians in amulets that would be placed in a person's tomb when they were buried. The Egyptians also believed that using hematite on injuries would stop the wounds from bleeding.

Some Native Americans would often grind this stone up into a powder to form a paste that they would then rub onto their bodies before they went into battle. They believed that by wearing the markings of the hematite crystal on their skin, they would become stronger and more powerful during the fight.

The hematite crystal is known for its ability to stabilize your energies and ground you. This stone works particularly well for those who practice forms of astral projection or other out-of-body experiences. Hematite works to protect you while your soul is journeying outside of your body; it anchors your body to that location so that you can return to it. Hematite also works by ensuring that no negative energies enter into your body while you are journeying.

Like amethyst, hematite is often the crystal of choice when you are trying to curb obsessive-compulsive disorders and various addictions, such as nicotine, alcohol, other drugs, and binge-eating. Hematite helps to provide mental clarity so that you can see your habits for what they truly are. It can improve your willpower so you will not give in to your temptations.

You can also use hematite when you need to focus or study. It helps center your thoughts so that you can become more focused on the task at hand. It improves your analytical abilities to find solutions to problems.

Hematite is used for its blood healing capabilities. It can help to improve circulatory health conditions. As well as various blood conditions, such as anemia and hemophilia. It does this by helping your kidneys filter blood more effectively.

If you have inflammation anywhere in your body, you should not use hematite for healing, as it can increase your redness. You should first wait for the inflammation to go down.

6
SPELLS

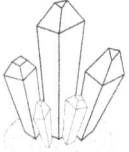

To start performing spells and magic, you will need to find a stone that resonates with the type of magic that you intend to perform. For some spells, you will need nothing more than the crystal you are working with. However, for other spells, you will require a candle that corresponds with your crystal, and sometimes various other items, such as a bowl, some thread, or a piece of paper.

Before you start with your spell, you should look at the different items that you will need in addition to your crystal to check if you have them in and around your house or in your crystal corner. Otherwise, you can buy them before you start your spellwork. Some spells need to be done at specific times, such as during a full moon, so it is best to ensure that you are prepared so that you do not have to wait for the next full moon before you can perform the spell.

Below, I have listed six quick and easy beginner spells that you can perform with the crystals you introduced in this book. As you continue to work with various other crystals, further your gem knowledge, and practice crystal magic, you will learn more advanced spells. Some crystal spells can be combined with a candle and herbal magic spells. To ensure that you get the most out of your stones, so I suggest you continue to practice your crystal magic and experiment with different spells and techniques!

Spell to Let Go of Pain and Unexpressed Emotions

This is an excellent spell that you can perform if you have recently lost someone or have been deeply hurt by somebody and are struggling to let go of the pain you are feeling. You can also use this spell if you are unable to express your emotions for any reason, like if you are a shy person. You find it difficult to share your feelings with other people or simply do not know how to describe how you are feeling.

You will be using a rose quartz crystal for this spell. It works by replacing any feelings and emotions that you might have bottled up, or any feelings of anger, grief, and frustration that you are feeling, with a calming energy. Through this, you can begin to heal any distress and heartache that you might be feeling or you can improve your communication to better express what you are currently feeling to other people. Doing so will make it so others can better understand you. This crystal can also help you process your feelings more positively and help you identify and heal any underlying issues that may have caused you grief.

For this spell, you will need the following items:

- 1 rose quartz crystal
- 1 pink candle

To begin this invocation, try to find an area that brings you comfort, and that is quiet, such as your crystal corner. When you are comfortable, light the candle and allow yourself to go into a meditative state, letting your consciousness float above the silence. Next, take your rose quartz crystal in your left hand (or place it over your heart for the spell to be more productive and open up your heart to accept healing).

You should meditate like this with the crystal in your hand for three minutes. Then you can start communicating with the crystal, either out loud or silently - whichever works for you. You should speak with your stone and state your intention, describing what has been upsetting you lately or what emotions you are finding difficult to express to others.

Once your inner thoughts are floating to the surface of your mind more freely. You are communicating with the stone more efficiently, you should start to think about why you are feeling this way and what you are struggling to come to terms with. You should not keep a hold of these emotions when they come to you, but rather let them pass through you as you continue to think about what has been bothering you about the occurrence.

When you finish communicating each of your emotions and memories with the crystal, you should visualize the memory as a picture. Imagine that you are letting the image float away into the distance. When you have done this, you should open yourself up to receive the soothing and healing energy of the crystal as it seeps into your body and flows through you. You can do so as you also accept the memory and look past it to your other memories.

If you have lost someone dear to you, then you should replace any painful memories with recollections of a happy time. This way, when you think of them the next time, you will associate them with happy memories and not the ones that hurt you.

When you have finished meditating and have gone through all of the feelings and emotions you have been experiencing, you should go outside and dig a hole in the dirt. Place your rose quartz into the hole and bury it. You should leave the stone in the ground for the rest of the day and the evening and take it out in the morning. You can repeat this spell as many times as you need to with the crystal.

Spell to Rid Yourself of Nightmares

If you are suffering from nightmares or night terrors, you can use this spell to rid yourself of them for good. It also works well for anyone that is having trouble sleeping or who wakes up often in the middle of the night. You should perform the spell before you go to bed in the evening and sleep with the crystal underneath your pillow to ensure you are receiving the best results.

In this spell, you will be using the citrine crystal to remove any bad dreams you are having to sleep better at night. You will, therefore, feel more rested in the morning. Citrine works by replacing the negative energy that surrounds your dreams with positive energy, providing you with pleasant dreams and improving your sleep quality.

For this spell, you will need the following items:

- 1 citrine crystal
- Material or cloth headband

To perform the spell, you should take a material or cloth headband and place the citrine crystal over your third eye chakra (on your forehead between your eyebrows). Place the headband over your head and adjust it atop the crystal so that it is secure.

Next, lie down on your back and focus on breathing in and out deeply three times. After this, you should visualize all the areas of your body where you feel tense, whether it is your neck, back, or legs.

Then, visualize light energy flooding into you from your feet upwards and replace the negative energy you identified when you envisioned the areas where you were tense. You should take your time to make sure you have gotten rid of all the negative, tight spaces in your body. If you need to, feel free to repeat this process until your body feels completely relaxed. There are no more tense areas, and then remove the headband and citrine from your forehead.

Next, place the citrine crystal underneath your pillow. When you go to bed that evening, you will notice that your dreams are more pleasant and that you can sleep more deeply.

Spell to Improve Fertility

Many people want to become parents, but some can find it difficult to fall pregnant. If you wish to conceive but are just not getting pregnant, this can put a lot of stress and pressure on you. This, in turn, can also make you less likely to conceive. This spell can help you to improve your fertility and increase the chance that you or your partner can become pregnant.

You will be using the moonstone in this spell. This stone can help you become more fertile and increase your chance of conceiving while also providing you with positive energy to decrease stress. This could be a factor as to why you are struggling to fall pregnant. It can also help remove any negative emotions and energies that you have experienced, such as fear and disappointment. The moonstone also provides protection to the expectant mother during her pregnancy.

For this spell, you will need the following items:

- 1 moonstone
- Needle and thread
- Article of clothing that you wear often
- A small square of green fabric

To begin this spell, put yourself into a meditative state, breathing in and out deeply, and hold the moonstone between your hands. Next, communicate with the stone and visualize your intentions and what you hope the outcome will be. Imagine that you or your partner are pregnant or that you are holding your newborn baby in your arms. Emit this visualization and the emotions you feel tied to this moment towards the moonstone.

When you have finished communicating with the moonstone, take the article of clothing that you have selected and fold it inside out. Then, find a place where you would like to attach the moonstone, such as on a piece of your clothing in a spot where it will not bother you when you wear it; this could be such on your arm or near the hem.

Next, place the fabric over the moonstone and then stitch it closed around the stone. While you are doing this, continue to visualize yourself becoming a parent. Once the material has been sewn closed, hold the item in your hands and say the following affirmation (or something similar): I welcome a child into my life.

When you have finished, put the item of clothing on and wear it for the rest of the day. You should not remove the stone until you have fallen pregnant, continuing to wear the clothing item regularly.

Spell to Increase Creativity

We all have creative energies flowing inside of us. However, there can be times when we are at a loss for what to create next. When you stare at an empty page, it can be a daunting task to create new art. This spell helps you to refocus your creative energies and will inspire you to get started with the current creative project at hand. Whether you are a writer, a painter, a musician, or even if you just want to feel creative, you will surely benefit from performing this spell.

For this spell, we will be using the carnelian stone. This stone promotes creativity and thinking. It can help you get through a creative block by removing any doubtful thoughts that you might be feeling. Then replace them with a sense that you can trust yourself, your intuitions, and your perceptions. This helps you to free your mind and become more creative in your endeavors.

For this spell, you will need the following items:

- 1 carnelian crystal
- Orange candle
- White paper
- Markers, crayons, paints, pencils, pens, or drawing pencils

First, sit down at a table and place a candle near where you will be working. Next, light the candle and pull out a piece of paper and any other creative instruments that you will be using for this spell. For example, suppose you are looking for more creativity in your writing. You will need a piece of paper and a pen, but if you are creating a piece of artwork, you will need your art supplies.

Next, place the carnelian crystal onto the sheet of paper and begin to write, paint, or draw on the page. It does not have to be anything in particular. You can start with a few keywords that you want to use or draw random shapes and objects. Allow yourself to freely write, paint, or draw without thinking about anything in particular.

I do not suggest that you stop this creative momentum. Instead, try to continue writing, drawing, or painting until you feel tired or complete your creative work. When you have finished, you can blow out the candle.

Next, pick up the writing, painting, or drawing you made and look at it in full. Then you can put the artwork up for display, throw it out, put it somewhere nobody else will see it, or place it somewhere to continue working on it at a later date.

Feel free to continue performing this spell whenever you feel that you do not have any inspiration to create something new. To boost your creativity before a big project, or whenever you want to make something without having any distractions to halt your creative flow.

Spell to Boost Your Confidence and Courage

This is a great spell to use if you are struggling to find courage in yourself to do or achieve something. To speak up for something that you believe in that others don't. Maybe you are being asked to do a presentation. Or attend a conference where you need to get up onto the stage and speak amongst a crowd of people. This spell helps to inspire more confidence in you and boost your courage so that you can get things done, make the right decisions, and walk up on stage with confidence to give the speech you have been preparing for.

For this spell, you will need the following items:

- 4 tiger's eye stones
- Red spell candle
- Small material bag

To perform this spell, sit down comfortably, place the candle in front of you, and allow yourself to go into a meditative state by breathing deeply and being in the present moment. Next, think of the event or occurrence that is coming up or make you feel nervous.

Then visualize the outcome that you would like to occur, whether it is finishing a project or walking up onto the stage with the confidence to win the day. You do not have to think specifically about any details. Try and communicate how you want the day or event to go about and how you are hoping to feel once you have completed it.

After you have visualized and communicated your feeling, light the candle, pick up one of the four tiger's eyes and place it in front of the candle as you say the following (or a similar) affirmation:

I will conquer my fears and find success.

Take the second tiger's eye, place it next to the previous tiger's eye in a line, and say something along the following lines:

I have confidence in what I am going to do and say.

Take the third tiger's eye and place it on the right-hand side of the candle. Then, say the following affirmation:

I know that I am able to communicate honestly and genuinely.

Finally, take the fourth tiger's eye and place it on the left-hand side of the candle. Say words such as these:

I will continue to support my decision no matter what other people think or say.

You should continue to meditate in this way and think of the events coming up or the conversation you are expecting to have with others. Visualize the outcome that you would like to happen and that you are successful in your endeavors. Do this until the candle burns out. You do not need to remain present during the time it takes for the candle to burn down; you can return to it after a while.

Once the candle has burned out, place the four tiger's eye stones inside a material bag and carry them along with you throughout your day and when the event occurs. To make this spell most effective, you should envision the protective qualities of the stones encompassing you while you are giving your presentation. Just as you are walking up onto the stage to give your speech and when you communicate with others.

Spell to Promote Self-Love, Self-Acceptance, and Self-Confidence

Self-love and confidence do not come easily for many people. Often, we do not understand what makes us love ourselves or what makes us confident. Some people believe that you cannot love yourself nor have confidence if nobody else appreciates or loves you or cannot be confident. It is the fact that you are not successful or have any accomplishments. However, this simply isn't true. We need to first love and accept ourselves before we can expect the same from other people.

You will be using the rose quartz crystal in this spell. With this crystal and its loving, healing properties, you can let go of any negative thoughts that you feel towards yourself and replace that energy with feelings of love and acceptance towards yourself. For this spell, it is recommended that you try to use a necklace or a bracelet that is made from rose quartz and also that you can use as a charm. If you do not have one, then you can also use rose quartz crystal.

For this spell, you will need the following items:

- 1 rose quartz crystal or a bracelet/necklace that has been made from rose quartz
- 1 pink candle
- 1 orange candle

To start the spell, you should place a pink and an orange candle next to each other and then place your rose quartz crystal, necklace, or bracelet in between them. Next, put yourself into a meditative state, light the pink candle and say the following affirmation, or something similar: My love for myself shines like the light from this candle.

Next, you will light the orange candle and say an affirmation similar to this: My self-acceptance shines like the light from this candle. Next, focus on the candles that you have lit as you pick up your rose quartz charm and hold it in your hands.

You will feel a shift in the energies surrounding you as you pick up your rose quartz charm. You should notice a sense of calm, loving, and acceptance seep into you as you hold the charm in your hands. You should visualize the love being absorbed into you as you open yourself up to these new energies.

Next, close your eyes, take a deep breath, and say the following affirmation, or something similar:

I accept myself as I am, I love myself, and I trust that I can do anything I set my mind to. Once you are done, you can blow out the candles and wear your charm or carry it in your pocket or bag to improve your self-confidence, self-love, and self-acceptance.

If you feel like the charm is no longer working as intended or has lost its potency and you are no longer feeling the effects of the spell, you can repeat this spell.

7

TALISMANS

Another way that you can perform crystal magic is through the use of talismans. A talisman can be anything from a small, tumbled stone, to a crystal amulet that you can wear around your neck or wrist. They are potent items that you can use to store magical energy. You can receive the benefits by merely carrying the talisman around with you throughout the day.

What makes these so powerful is that they are imbued with your magical intention. Working to ensure that you are meeting all of the outcomes that you are envisioning for yourself.

It can become even more powerful when you think about the talisman that you are wearing or carrying. Your magical intentions will resonate deeply within the object to increase your communication with it. This will also help you remember what it is that you are trying to accomplish.

People will often use a talisman when they try to reach a goal or an outcome for a short-term duration. For instance, when they need to improve their focus and concentration to ace an exam. Another time people use talismans is when they need to boost their confidence for a presentation or event that is coming up.

However, you can also use talismans to improve yourself or provide you with healing over a more extended time. Some examples include giving up an addiction like smoking, which can take some time, or remove any negative energy that might surround you daily and replace them with positive, healing energies.

If you are taking a talisman along with you throughout the day in your pocket or bag, you should ensure that you choose an object that will not get damaged easily. Tumbled or polished stones and crystals can be more susceptible to damage, especially if you forget that your stone or crystal is in a specific spot. You place a sharp object near it.

However, it is often more desirable to carry a tumbled or polished stone or crystal. They are energy amplifiers and can be much more effective when infused with magical intention. In this case, you should keep the stone or crystal in a place where you will not put anything with it. Such as in your back pocket or in an unused pouch in your bag.

You could also consider covering or wrapping up the stone or crystal with a cloth. However, many people feel that if you wrap something around it, it will not work as effectively. So, if you place your talisman somewhere you do not use or go into often, you should not have to worry about covering it or wrapping it up.

To charge an item, stone, or crystal as a talisman, you will need the following items:

- 1 black, purple, or white candle
- 1 or more basic quartz or amethyst crystals

- 1 item, stone, or crystal that will be used as your talisman

To start charging your talisman, you should place the candle in front of you and put your basic quartz or amethyst crystals that you will be using in front of it. Next, light the candle and hold the talisman that needs to be charged in between your hands. You should remember that you have to use an item, stone, or crystal as your talisman; you can also use a pendant or bracelet with a gemstone in it.

Next, get yourself into a meditative state and close your eyes as you breathe in and out deeply. You should then think of what you want the talisman to do for you, your intentions, and what possible outcome you are hoping for. You are welcome to communicate out loud with your talisman or quietly in your head - whichever you are most comfortable with.

Next, you should speak your affirmations with your talisman to help you communicate your intentions with the stone. Below are a few examples of the affirmations that you can say for some different situations. As you continue with your magical crystal journey, you will learn various affirmations for the different situations you will face. You will be able to charge your crystal however you see fit.

You should always remember that these affirmations are just examples, and you can use any words that you feel are right for you. Once you have completed your affirmations and sense that your stone or crystal has been programmed according to your intentions, you should leave your talisman with your charging crystals in front of the candle. Allow the candle to continue to burn for one hour.

After an hour has passed, blow out the candle. Take your crystal with you so that it can continue to fill you with the desire to reach your outcome and with protective, healing, balancing, or encouraging energies that you charged it with.

Energy Balance

To charge a talisman to help you balance your energies, you can utilize either a jade or malachite crystal. If you are using a malachite crystal, then you should use it in its tumbled or polished form, unless you have experience working with the crystal. You can use this talisman to fill you with soothing light, stabilizing your energies, and healing you from within.

Once you have lit your candle and placed your charging crystals down in front of them, hold the jade or malachite between your hands. Begin to meditate as you visualize your intentions and a soothing green light filling you with peace and healing you from the inside out. Starting from the tips of your fingers all the way to the soles of your feet.

During this time, try not to think about why you are feeling this way. You might provide your talisman with the wrong intentions, and it will not function as effectively as it should.

Continue to meditate and focus on the calming and peaceful energies swirling around your body. Once you are more relaxed and in tune with yourself, say the following affirmation, or something similar: I am healed. My energies have been rebalanced from what previously unsettled me.

Protection

To charge a talisman to protect you, you can opt for a bloodstone or a jet crystal. You can use this talisman to provide you with protection in any situation where you do not feel safe or feel negative energies are surrounding you. This stone will replace these negative energies with positive ones.

Once you have lit your candle, place your charging crystals down in front of them. Hold the bloodstone or the jet crystal in between your hands and begin to meditate as you visualize your body being filled with a warm white light. Observe as it seeps in from the tips of your fingers to the soles of your feet.

Next, welcome this white light into your life and replace any negative energy inside you and your surroundings. Associate this light with positive, protective energies that form a shield around you. When you are ready, say an affirmation similar to the following: The white light from this candle protects me and shields me from the negative energies that try to come into my life.

Money

To charge a talisman to help you become wealthier, you can use either a citrine or a jade crystal. You can use this talisman to help you generate more money and wealth in your life and help you increase your financial stability.

Once you have lit your candle and placed your charging crystals, hold your chosen crystal in between your hands. Begin to meditate as you think of your intentions, what you would like to accomplish.

If you are performing this spell to get out of debt, try not to think about the debt that you are in during this time. This includes or even how you are going to increase your wealth. Instead, focus on visualizing yourself, making and saving money, and concentrate on the feelings that you associate with these thoughts. If there is something you are saving money for, think about how much money you need to have to accomplish your goals. Visualize yourself working toward making that money.

Next, visualize the candle's light filling you up and a slow burn growing inside of you, pushing you to become more successful and encouraging you to make and save more money. Then visualize this light, removing any feelings of doubt and uncertainty from your body, replacing it with confidence, encouragement, and the perseverance to not give up.

Next, say the following affirmation, or something similar: I will earn and save more money to become wealthier and more financially stable.

Health

To charge a talisman to help you improve your health, select any healing stone you prefer. This can be amethyst, basic quartz, bloodstone, citrine, lapis lazuli, and rose quartz. If there are other healing crystals that you know of or use often, then you can use those, too. This talisman can help improve your health, reduce your risks of developing health conditions. It may even, or help to treat current health conditions that you might be suffering from.

Once you have lit your candle and placed your charging crystals, hold your chosen healing crystal in between your hands. Begin to meditate as you think about your intentions, the outcome you would like, and how you would like the crystal to work with you to provide healing benefits.

Next, visualize the light of the candle filling you up with soothing, healing energy. Imagine this light moving around throughout your body, and focus on the areas where you are either experiencing pain or where you feel the problem lies. For example, if you feel pain in your leg, focus on healing the discomfort you feel there. Then, imagine the light removing the pain and dark energies that you are feeling in that area. You can continue to visualize this until your body feels more relaxed, and you sense that the light has thoroughly worked its way through your body.

Next, say the following affirmation, or something similar: With the light of this candle, my body has been healed of any health condition that ails me. I am filled with a soothing, calming energy.

CONCLUSION

Crystals have been used in cultures the world over for thousands of years. They have been utilized in a variety of ways, such as in magical practices, in religious and spiritual ceremonies, protective charms, jewelry, amulets, talismans, decorative ornaments, as war paint and makeup, and even in medicinal concoctions. These stones have retained most of their properties and attributes. These characteristics were first described and assigned to them in ancient times. Some beliefs that no longer make sense in today's knowledgeable world and some that were bad for a person's health have been replaced, such as powdered malachite.

In today's modern age, we have given new meaning to crystals and magic through Wiccan beliefs and our interest in spirituality and the occult. We also use crystals in many new ways that had not been thought of in the past. Various new technologies like radios, ultrasounds, watches, and computer chips all use crystals to transmit and receive energies so that they can function.

Some crystals are more popular and easier to find than others. This includes the basic clear quartz, rose quartz, amethyst, citrine, moonstone, carnelian, bloodstone, jade, lapis lazuli, malachite, tiger's eye, jet, and hematite. There are hundreds of more different crystals that you can buy. Still, I recommend that you buy a variety of these common ones first and get a feel for practicing spells and magic before moving on to other crystals. These common crystals can get you started with practicing magic and charms while still sticking to a budget.

There are hundreds of different crystals that you can first buy when you start your collection. While it might seem daunting or overwhelming at first, choosing a crystal is unlike anything you have experienced before. As you stand in the store and run your hands over the crystals, you will feel the pull at you, guiding you towards the stone that has decided to choose you to bestow its gifts upon. Try and open yourself up to communicating with all of the crystals available and welcoming all that guide you until you have found the one that is the right fit for you.

Before a crystal makes its way to you, it goes on a long journey. Many people will have handled your crystal before you. They might have had negative energies that were absorbed into the stone or different intentions to yours. Because of this, you should always ensure that you cleanse your chosen crystals when you get home to remove any of these intentions and negative energies from the stone. This will make it so you can program and activate the crystal to work for you. If you do not do this, then your crystal will not be as powerful in the spells that you cast, nor will they provide you with the properties and attributes you were hoping for. This will likely leave you disappointed.

When buying crystals, you should also check to see if it is projective, receptive, or both. A projective crystal is mostly used in magic that is directed towards something or at someone else. It helps to improve certain qualities of yourself. An example of a projective crystal is citrine, which can help to improve depression. It also can assist you in becoming motivated and creative. Citrine is also a healing crystal. It is a projective stone that can be used to provide health benefits to someone else.

In contrast, receptive stones are used in magic to heal your body, mind, and soul. These stones help you stabilize the energy that is flowing inside your body and focus on healing you from the inside out. An example of a receptive stone is the amethyst. It is often used to help manage obsessive-compulsive disorders and can also help people curb addictions. Additionally, it provides the person who is wearing or using it with calm energies to stabilize their emotions.

I have included a few spells that can get you started with using crystals in magic. Once you have mastered these spells, you can move on to more complex spells. After you begin using crystals for their various properties and attributes, it is easy to continue to use them more in various aspects of your life.

REFERENCES

A Brief History of Crystals and Healing. (n.d.). Crystalage. https://www.crystalage.com/crystal_information/crystal_history/

A list of Gemstone Birthstones And Astrology. (2020, July 5). Gem Rock Auctions. https://www.gemrockauctions.com/learn/additional-gemstone-information/a-list-of-gemstone-birthstones-and-astrology

Amethyst. (n.d.). Origin Stones. https://originstones.com/project/amethyst/

Amethyst History and Lore. (n.d.). Gemological Institute of America. https://www.gia.edu/amethyst-history-lore

Basic Paganism Beliefs: What DO Pagans Believe? (2019, February 18). Otherworldly Oracle. https://otherworldlyoracle.com/basic-paganism-beliefs-what-do-pagans-believe/

Bloodstone Meaning, Powers and History. (n.d.). Jewels for Me. https://www.jewelsforme.com/gem_and_jewelry_library/bloodstone#:~:text=Legend%20says%20bloodstone%20was%20formed

References

Bloodstone Overview. (n.d.). American Gem Society. https://www.americangemsociety.org/page/bloodstoneoverview

Braid, F. (n.d.). Lapis Lazuli Symbolism. International Gem Society. https://www.gemsociety.org/article/history-legend-lapis-lazuli-gems-yore/

Carnelian: History and Healing Stone Properties. (n.d.). Emmanuelle Guyon. https://www.en.emmanuelleguyon.com/vertus_cornaline_en.html

Chamberlain, L. (2018). Wicca Spellbook Starter Kit: A Book of Candle, Crystal, and Herbal Spells. Chamberlain Publications.

Crowl, C. (2019, July 11). Projective and Receptive Energies in Crystals and Gemstones. Charlotte Crowl. https://www.charlottecrowl.com/post/projective-and-receptive-energies-in-crystals-and-gemstones

Crystalline Light. (2015). Heat Treated Citrine vs Natural Citrine [YouTube Video]. On YouTube. https://www.youtube.com/watch?v=nA2Q_I3Id7U

Crystals Rocks Minerals | Understanding the Difference. (n.d.). Stone Mania. https://www.stonemania.co.uk/blog/difference-between-rocks-and-minerals

Difference Between Rocks and Stones. (n.d.). Difference Between. http://www.differencebetween.net/science/nature/difference-between-rocks-and-stones/

Earle, S. (n.d.). 1.4 Minerals and Rocks. BC Open Textbooks. https://opentextbc.ca/geology/chapter/1-4-minerals-and-rocks/#:~:text=A%20mineral%20is%20a%20pure,halite%2C%20calcite%2C%20

and%20amphibole.

Faragher, A. K. (2018, April 9). A Beginner's Guide to Healing Crystals and Harnessing Their Energy. Allure. https://www.allure.com/story/magickal-healing-crystals-guide

Ferrell, S. (2016, June 26). How Crystals Are Used in Modern Times. Trinity Healing. https://www.trinityhealingconnection.com/post/2016/06/26/how-crystals-are-used-in-modern-times#:~:text=Sonar%2C%20ultrasound%2C%20radios%2C%20transistors

Gems, L. (2019, August 30). Duality & Wholeness – Magic of Receptive and Projective Gemstones. Gems In Style. https://gemsinstyle.com/blogs/news/duality-that-creates-wholeness-magic-of-receptive-and-projective-gemstones

Gemstone Properties. (n.d.). Witch's Cauldron. http://www.witchscauldron.net/cauldron/stones.htm

Gemstones & Signs of the Zodiac. (n.d.). IvyRose Holistic. https://www.ivyroses.com/Crystals/Crystals_ZodiacSigns.php

Gerbis, N. (n.d.). How Are Crystals Made? How Stuff Works. https://science.howstuffworks.com/environmental/earth/geology/how-are-crystals-made.htm

Gottesman, D. S., & Gottesman, R. L. (n.d.). Three Types of Rock. American Museum of Natural History. https://www.amnh.org/exhibitions/permanent/planet-earth/how-do-we-read-the-rocks/three-types-of-rock#:~:text=There%20are%20three%20kinds%20of

Hall, J. (2009). The Crystal Bible Volume 1: The Definitive Guide to Over 200 Crystals. Godsfield Press Ltd.

Harrison, M. (2019, November 7). An In-Depth Look at the History of Crystals and Healing. Cosmic Cuts. https://cosmiccuts.com/blogs/healing-stones-blog/an-in-depth-look-at-the-history-of-crystals-and-healing

Hematite. (n.d.). Origin Stones. https://originstones.com/project/hematite/

Hematite Meaning, Powers and History. (n.d.). Jewels for Me. https://www.jewelsforme.com/gem_and_jewelry_library/hematite#:~:text=Birthstone

%20Jewelry-

How Do Crystals Form & Grow? (2016, March 11). Geology Page. http://www.geologypage.com/2016/03/how-do-crystals-form-grow.html

Hughes, J. J. (2019, June 26). Crystal Use - Through the Ages. Goodreads. https://www.goodreads.com/author_blog_posts/18519400-crystal-use---through-the-ages

Jade History and Lore. (n.d.). Gemological Institute of America. https://www.gia.edu/jade-history-lore

Jadeite Jade Quality Factors. (n.d.). Gemological Institute of America. https://www.gia.edu/jade-quality-factor

Jaw-Dropping Facts. (2019). 8 Weird Facts About Ancient Egypt Makeup and Ancient Cosmetics History [YouTube Video]. In YouTube. https://www.youtube.com/watch?v=mRyqqdD7ZcI

Jet. (n.d.). Peaceful Mind. https://www.peacefulmind.com/crystals/metaphysical-properties/jet-properties/

King, H. M. (n.d.). Geodes. Geology. https://geology.com/articles/geodes/

Lapis Meaning, Powers and History. (n.d.). Jewels for Me. https://www.jewelsforme.com/gem_and_jewelry_library/lapis

Malachite. (n.d.). Origin Stones. https://originstones.com/project/malachite/

Malachite Meaning, Powers and History. (n.d.). Jewels for Me. https://www.jewelsforme.com/gem_and_jewelry_library/malachite#:~:text=The%

20name%20malachite%20derives%20from

March Birthstone. (n.d.). Gemological Institute of America. https://www.gia.edu/birthstones/march-birthstones

Minerals, Crystals, Rocks & Stones: What's the Difference? (n.d.). FossilEra. https://www.fossilera.com/pages/minerals-crystals-rocks-stones-what-s-the-difference

Moonstone. (n.d.). Origin Stones. https://originstones.com/project/moonstone/

Moonstone History and Lore. (n.d.). Gemological Institute of America. https://www.gia.edu/moonstone-history-lore

Moonstone in Ancient Lore and Legends. (2016, November 30). Moon Magic. https://moonmagic.com/blogs/news/moonstone-in-ancient-lore-and-legends#:~:text=Moonstone%20is%20the%20sacred%20stone

Nephrite vs. Jadeite: What's the Difference? (n.d.). Beadworks Norwalk. https://beadworksnorwalk.com/whats-difference-nephrite-jadeite/

Projective Stones. (n.d.). The Witch Depot. https://the-witch-depot.myshopify.com/pages/projective-stones

Quartz. (n.d.). Origin Stones. https://originstones.com/project/quartz/

Quartz Crystal Meaning, Types, History & Healing Properties. (n.d.). AP Crystals. https://apcrystals.com/blogs/crystal-blog/quartz-crystal-meaning-history-and-healing-properties

Receptive Energy. (n.d.). The Witch Depot. https://the-witch-depot.myshopify.com/pages/receptive-energy

Rose Quartz. (n.d.). Origin Stones. https://originstones.com/project/rose-quartz/

Rose Quartz History and Lore. (n.d.). Gemological Institute of America. https://www.gia.edu/rose-quartz-history-lore#:~:text=Rose%20quartz%20jewelry%20was%20known

Science for Kids: Crystals. (n.d.). Ducksters. https://www.ducksters.com/science/crystals.php#:~:text=Crystals%20often%20form%20in%20nature

Shine, T. (2018, September 19). A Beginner's Guide to Clearing, Cleansing, and Charging Crystals. Healthline. https://www.healthline.com/health/how-to-cleanse-crystals

Stone Energies. (n.d.). Tryskelion. http://www.tryskelion.com/stones_stoneneg.html

The Most Powerful Crystals for Your Zodiac Sign. (2019, April 10). Horoscope.Com. https://www.horoscope.com/article/the-most-powerful-crystals-for-your-zodiac-sign-html/

The Tricky Bits … Atoms, Molecules and the Rest. (n.d.). Oxford University Museum of Natural History. https://www.oum.ox.ac.uk/thezone/minerals/define/chemical.htm#:~:text=They%20are%20all%20naturally%20occurring

Tiger Eye History. (2015, September 11). Aurum Brothers. https://aurumbrothers.com/blogs/history-of-our-stones/44290817-tiger-eye-history

Tiger Eye: History and Healing Properties. (n.d.). Emmanuelle Guyon. https://www.en.emmanuelleguyon.com/vertus_oeil_de_tigre_en.html#:~:text=Tiger%

20eye%20was%20discovered%20in

What Is a Mineral? (n.d.). Oxford University Museum of Natural History. https://www.oum.ox.ac.uk/thezone/minerals/define/index.htm

What Is Jade? The Difference Between Jadeite and Nephrite. (n.d.). Jadeite Atelier. https://www.jadeite-atelier.com/blogs/jade-articles/what-is-jade-jadeite-and-nephrite

What Is the Difference Between a Rock and a Mineral? (n.d.). United States Geological Survey. https://www.usgs.gov/faqs/what-difference-between-a-rock-and-a-mineral?qt-news_science_products=0#qt-news_science_products

ABOUT THE AUTHOR

Monique Joiner Siedlak: Author, Witch, Warrior.

With storytelling infused with mysticism, modern paganism, and new age spirituality, Monique awakens your potential. Initiated into the craft at 20, her 80+ books explore the magick and mysteries of life.

A Long Island native, she now calls Southeast Poland home but remains a citizen of Mother Earth.

Beyond her pen, Monique craves new experiences and cherishes nature, advocating for animal welfare.

Join her captivating journey as she transports you to enchanting realms and empowers your own transformative path. Unleash the dormant magic within and embrace the extraordinary with Monique Joiner Siedlak's evocative words.

To find out more about Monique artistically, spiritually, and personally, feel free to visit her **official website**.

www.mojosiedlak.com

- facebook.com/mojosiedlak
- x.com/mojosiedlak
- instagram.com/mojosiedlak
- youtube.com/@MoniqueJoinerSiedlak_Author
- tiktok.com/@mojosiedlak
- bookbub.com/authors/monique-joiner-siedlak
- pinterest.com/mojosiedlak

African Spirituality Beliefs and Practices

Hoodoo

Seven African Powers: The Orishas

Cooking for the Orishas

Lucumi: The Ways of Santeria

Voodoo of Louisiana

Haitian Vodou

Orishas of Trinidad

Connecting with your Ancestors

Blood Magick

The Orishas

Vodun: West Africa's Spiritual Life

Marie Laveau: Life of a Voodoo Queen

Candomblé: Dancing for the God

Umbanda

Exploring the Rich and Diverse World

Divination Magic for Beginners

Divination with Runes

Divination with Diloggún

Divination with Osteomancy

Divination with the Tarot

Divination with Stones

The Beginner's Guide to Inner Growth

Astral Projection for Beginners

Meditation for Beginners

Reiki for Beginners

Mastering Your Inner Potential

Creative Visualization

Manifesting With the Law of Attraction

Holistic Healing and Energy

Healing Animals with Reiki

Crystal Healing

Communicating with Your Spirit Guides

Empathic Understanding and Enlightenment

Being an Empath Today

Life on Fire

Healing Your Inner Child

Change Your Life

Raising Your Vibe

The Indie Author's Guides

The Indie Author's Guide to Fast Drafting Your Novel

Get a Handle on Life

Get a Handle on Stress

Time Bound

Get a Handle on Anxiety

Get a Handle on Depression

Get a Handle on Procrastination

The Holistic Yoga and Wellness Series

Yoga for Beginners

Yoga for Stress

Yoga for Back Pain

Yoga for Weight Loss

Yoga for Flexibility

Yoga for Advanced Beginners

Yoga for Fitness

Yoga for Runners

Yoga for Energy

Yoga for Your Sex Life

Yoga to Beat Depression and Anxiety

Yoga for Menstruation

Yoga to Detox Your Body

Yoga to Tone Your Body

The DIY Body Care Series

Creating Your Own Body Butter

Creating Your Own Body Scrub

Creating Your Own Body Spray

SUPPORT ME BY LEAVING A REVIEW!

goodreads

www.ingramcontent.com/pod-product-compliance
Lightning Source LLC
Chambersburg PA
CBHW071955070426
42453CB00008BA/800